YOUNG, BLACK, AND DETERMINED:

A Biography of Lorraine Hansberry

YOUNG, BLACK, AND DETERMINED:

A Biography of Lorraine Hansberry

BY PATRICIA C. McKISSACK
AND FREDRICK L. McKISSACK

HOLIDAY HOUSE/NEW YORK

To Sandra Walton

P.C.M.

F.L.M.

Library of Congress Cataloging-in-Publication Data
McKissack, Pat, 1944–
Young, Black, and Determined: a biography of Lorraine Hansberry/
by Patricia C. McKissack and Fredrick L. McKissack. — 1st ed.
p.   cm
Includes bibliographical references (p. 145) and index.
Summary: A biography of the black playwright who received great
recognition for her work at an early age.
ISBN 0-8234-1300-4 (reinforced)
1. Hansberry, Lorraine, 1930–1965 — Biography — Juvenile literature.
2. Dramatists, American —20th century—Biography—Juvenile literature.
[1. Hansberry, Lorraine, 1930–1965. 2. Dramatists, American.
3. Afro-Americans — Biography. 4. Women — Biography.]
I. McKissack, Fredrick. II. Title.
PS3515.A515Z77   1998   97-2084   CIP   AC
812'.54 — dc21
[B]

ACKNOWLEDGMENTS

We owe a debt of gratitude to a number of people who helped us complete this project. It was a joy talking for hours to Mamie Hansberry Mitchell, who shared so much of her sister's life with us, especially the early years. We appreciate the input of scholars such as Jewell Gresham Nemiroff and Margaret Wilkerson who read our manuscript and offered suggestions and corrections. Lorraine's friends and colleagues, Ossie Davis and Ruby Dee, were also helpful. Without Bill Rice, one of the best photo researchers in the business, this would still be a work in process. We'd also like to express our sincere thanks to Basil Phillips of Johnson Publishing Co. Inc. whose friendship and support throughout the years have been unfailing. And finally, we'd like to acknowledge the outstanding editorial guidance of Regina Griffin and the enthusiasm of the entire staff at Holiday House. More thanks to all others who helped along the way, especially our family. Lorraine Hansberry's story would not be available to young readers if it were not for you.

TABLE OF CONTENTS

CHAPTER 1

YOUNG . . .

For some time now — I think since I was a child — I have been possessed of the desire to put down the stuff of my life. That is a commonplace impulse, apparently, among persons of massive self-interest; sooner or later we all do it. And I am quite certain, there is only one internal quarrel: how much of the truth to tell? How much, how much, how much!

LORRAINE HANSBERRY

1

1930.

The Great Depression had begun.

1930.

That year more than 1,300 United States banks closed due to the stock market crash of 1929. Four million American workers were thrown out of work. People lost their homes and businesses, and to make matters worse, the Midwest was ravaged by a drought. Even before the Depression started, a large number of African Americans were already unemployed and undereducated, living in unsafe, substandard housing. Yet, even though times were hard and their futures didn't look too bright, black people still got married and started families.

A breadline during the
Great Depression

Their children listened to *The Lone Ranger* and *Lum 'n Abner* on the radio or slipped under a fence to catch a glimpse of Josh Gibson or Satchel Paige playing in a Negro League baseball game. Their teenage sons and daughters rolled back the rugs and danced to Fats Waller's Broadway hit *Ain't Misbehavin'*, or slipped a kiss in a dark theater while watching the Academy Award-winning movie *All Quiet on the Western Front*. Life went on.

1930.

Midway through that year Lorraine Vivian Hansberry was born at Provident Medical Center on the South Side of Chicago, a hospital founded by a prominent African-American physician, Dr. Daniel Hale Williams. In 1893 Dr. Williams had shocked the world and made medical history by performing the first successful open-heart surgery.

The Hansberrys were proud of their African heritage and passed that pride on to their daughter the day she was born. Lorraine's birth certificate provides the usual vital statistics:

Date of Birth: May 19, 1930
Sex: Female
Father: Carl Hansberry, age 33, employed as a deputy marshal
Mother: Nannie Hansberry, age 32, committeewoman

But there is also a very noticeable correction on her birth certificate. In the space for "color" (meaning race), "Negro" was crossed out and replaced with a "B" for Black. Carl and Nannie Hansberry insisted upon this correction, even though, at the time, most African Americans preferred to be called "Negro." The prevailing newspaper style of the day was to spell Negro with a small letter, which was insulting to many African Americans. Later in the year, black people felt they had scored a victory when the prestigious *New York Times* agreed to capitalize the word, but Carl Hansberry was not impressed.

What Lorraine's birth certificate doesn't show is her family's long history and tradition of hard work and literacy. Lorraine's paternal great-grandfather, William Hansberry, was born a slave in Culpepper County, Virginia, the son of an African woman and her master, whose name was Hansberry. When William was about fifteen, his father-master sold him to the Young family in Clinton, Louisiana. William could read and write, which was very unusual in the 1850s, since it was illegal in most states for a slave to be educated. More importantly, William was a skilled craftsman who was hired out by his master to serve as foreman on construction jobs in the area. According to Clinton historical records, William Hansberry made the bricks for the local courthouse and the Methodist Church.

Toward the close of the Civil War, when Union troops were advancing on Clinton, William's master secretly gathered all the Young family's silver, gold, and jewels, and, with William's help, hid the treasure in the woods. Young was later killed trying to escape through Union lines. After the war ended, William retrieved the treasure without guilt. He saw it as all the back pay due him for the hard work he'd done during slavery. William prudently kept the source of his wealth a secret and carefully managed it so as not to raise suspicion. He gradually used his money to buy 670 acres of land in Felicia Parish, a rural area outside Clinton. Some of the original land is still owned by his descendants.

Not much is known about William's wife, but they had ten children. One of their three sons, Mender Hansberry, used his inheritance to study at Alcorn College in Mississippi, where he later taught. Mender married Ethel Frances Woodward from Jackson, Mississippi, also a graduate of Alcorn, and they had six children. Two of their sons were William Leo Hansberry, who became a well-known African scholar, and Lorraine's father, Carl Hansberry, who became a successful businessman.

Clearly, William Hansberry's legacy was not just money and property, but a love of knowledge, a desire for self-improvement through education, and a willingness to work hard.

Through her mother, Nannie Perry, Lorraine's family tree can be traced back to her grandfather George Perry, a slave. At age twelve, he escaped from his master in Tennessee and made his way to New York City. There, he worked for a theater company and saved every penny, except for what it cost to pay a tutor to teach him how to read and write. Once he learned the basics, George was able to continue on his own. In time, he earned enough money to return to Tennessee, where he bought his and his mother's freedom before the Civil War.

After the war, George married Charlotte Organ, an African-Cherokee woman, and they settled in Columbia, Tennessee, and raised six children. One of their daughters was Lorraine's mother, Nannie.

George Perry's legacy was one of courage, persistence, and determination. It is ironic that almost a hundred years later, George Perry's granddaughter would make her own escape of sorts to New York City to realize her dreams, and that she, too, would earn a living in the theater.

Like so many Southern-born blacks seeking relief from cruel and often violent Southern racism and discrimination, Carl and Nannie migrated to Chicago during World War I and settled on the South Side. The two of them met at a social function, and, after a brief courtship, married. Working together, the Hansberrys had been able to build a thriving real estate business, buying apartment buildings and dividing them into "kitchenettes," one large room and a kitchen, similar to present-day efficiency, or studio, apartments.

By the time Lorraine was born, Carl Hansberry was one of the largest landlords on the South Side, prosperous and influential. Lorraine's birth — even at the onset of the Depression — placed no financial burden on her family, the way it might have on some of their neighbors. The new baby was a welcome addition to the large and comfortable Hansberry home at 5330 Calumet Avenue.

Lorraine was the fourth and youngest child. Her older brothers, Carl, Jr. and Perry, were twelve and ten years old, and her sister, Mamie, was seven.

As is often the case with older and younger siblings, each one views the past from a different point of view. For example, Mamie Mitchell, Lorraine's older sister, who presently lives in Los Angeles, California, remembers Lorraine as the "baby," always being pampered, indulged, and loved. "She was like a beautiful little doll to us," remembered Mamie. "Mother hardly had anything to do for her. I did it all."

Lorraine, however, reflected on her childhood from a different perspective. In a collection of her autobiographical writings, entitled *To Be Young, Gifted and Black,* Lorraine wrote:

The last born is an object toy which comes in years when brothers and sisters who are seven, ten, twelve years older are old enough to appreciate it rather than poke out its eyes. They do not mind diapering you the first two years, but by the time you are five you are a pest that has to be attended to in the washroom, taken to the movies and "sat with" at night. You are not a person — you are a nuisance who is not particular fun any more.

In spite of her birth order, Lorraine was a healthy, happy infant. From her parents she received love and security and a remarkable family history. Lorraine's ancestors provided her with splendid examples of how to overcome adversity through courage, discipline, persistence, and commitment. As she grew up, these qualities helped shape her character as well.

2

Chicago's South Side neighborhoods have changed considerably since Lorraine was a girl playing hopscotch on the sidewalks. The South Side was shaped roughly like a triangle. Its northernmost point was 12th Street, where the bus and train stations were located. During the Depression a steady stream of African Americans from all points South arrived there daily. The new arrivals, filled with hopes for a better life for themselves and their children, flocked to the South Side where friends and relatives from "down home" welcomed them.

At the base of the South Side triangle were all-white neighborhoods. Black people from all socio-economic levels lived within the segregated area known as the South Side "Black Belt," which was one of the largest black urban communities in the country. There were class divisions within the community based on education and

The South Side of Chicago in 1941

economic criteria. College-trained professional, high income translated into high social status; poor education, low income meant low status.

Although the residents of the Black Belt moved in different social circles, they were forced by segregation to share the same neighborhoods. It was not uncommon for a college graduate to live across the street from a school dropout. A racketeer often lived a few apartments away from a preacher. A domestic worker might live next door to a woman with a maid of her own.

Mothers in the community united in their common concern for their children and education. They attended PTA meetings and might complain to a principal — who probably lived in an apartment only a few blocks away — that the class sizes were too large and the books were outdated; the fathers — one perhaps a Pullman Car porter and the other a doctor — went to the black Elks' lodge, where after a brief business meeting, the men would sit around and voice their opinions about why the nation was in trouble, and how, if given a chance, they had a plan to fix it; children played hopscotch and tag together in the park, shared dill pickles that reeked of garlic, and fought over who said what about whom.

A number of major businesses that served the Black Belt were owned and managed by whites. In 1930 and '31 black South Siders held strikes against white businesses that didn't hire black workers. The strike resulted in the placement of several hundred blacks in jobs that had not been available to them before.

There was also a wide assortment of bustling, albeit struggling, black-owned businesses, and an equal number of churches, funeral parlors, liquor stores, and taverns positioned where one could buy a half-pint of whiskey, get shot, and hold the funeral services all at one intersection.

Since Carl Hansberry was a successful businessman and a prominent community leader, he was part of the upper class. It is not known when Lorraine became aware of the class system that existed in the Black Belt, but she instinctively rejected the notion, long before she was able to explain why. Lorraine's feelings of frustration were common among black children from advantaged families who lived in a disadvantaged community such as the Black Belt. The whole orientation of the black upper class was to "better the race" through education and business enterprise, which set them apart from the poor and uneducated masses.

Although Carl taught Lorraine that she wasn't better than anybody else, except those, such as bigots and racists, who told her she wasn't, Lorraine was still expected to speak and act in a manner befitting her class. She never liked the feeling of being separated from other children, so she grew to resent her family's affluence.

Many years later, when people said that her father had "amassed a fortune," Lorraine tried to explain that it was not true. Black fortunes, she argued, were measured in the thousands of dollars rather than millions, adding this qualifying statement: ". . . relative to American society of the Nineteen Thirties and Forties Carl A. Hansberry had simply become a reasonably successful businessman of the middle class."

3

Lorraine's earliest memories are of playing games with children in her neighborhood. There was a nonsense rhyme repeated to a hand-clapping rhythm that she liked very much, because in a small way it allowed her to share the world of the streetwise girls.

> *Oh, Mary, Mack, Mack, Mack*
> *All dressed in black, black, black,*
> *With silver buttons, buttons, buttons*
> *All down her back, back, back.*
> *She asked her mother, mother, mother*
> *For fifteen cents, cents, cents,*
> *To see the elephant, elephant, elephant*
> *Jump the fence, fence, fence.*
> *Well, he jumped so high, high, high,*
> *'Til he touched the sky, sky, sky*
> *And he didn't come back, back, back*
> *'Til the fourth of Ju-ly, ly, ly.*

Lorraine Hansberry, at about age 5

The "ly" (lie) was always emphasized, because "lie" was considered a word "nice" children from "good homes" didn't use. For Lorraine to call someone "a lie" would have been "common." But Lorraine sang the forbidden word at the top of her voice, a small act of rebellion against class distinctions.

Lorraine marked the start of her own rebellion from another incident. Nothing helped to draw the class lines clearer, or define her "apartness" more, than a white fur coat she was given on her fifth Christmas.

In her own words this is what happened:

> *Because it was the largest, most finely wrapped of all the boxes, she had noticed it for days. And when, at last, the morning came and she was allowed to rip asunder the smooth white tissue paper and see what lay inside, the child could do nothing but sit stunned.*
> *The grown-ups ohhhed and ahhhed around her.*
> *They congratulated the mother.*
> *They insisted that the outfit be put, at once, upon the child.*
> *They touched the fur and exclaimed afresh with passion.*
> *And all the while the child sat half ill with the outrage that had been committed against her Christmas. She was compelled to stand up, a small angry mannequin in her pajamas, while the coat was first lovingly shaken and then thrust upon her frame and buttoned to her chin quite as if she was about to go out into the cold. Then the muff was placed on her fists, and the scratching little cap on her brow.*

At that time many schools in the Chicago area had two terms, one starting in September and the other in January. Lorraine entered kindergarten at the beginning of the new year. "My mother sent me to kindergarten in white fur in the middle of the Depression," she explained with a strong tinge of resentment: "The kids beat me up; and I think it was from that moment I became a rebel . . ."

Lorraine described another childhood memory in her autobiographical journal. When the hot summer sun heated up the brick tenements, the children got fussy and whiny. Seeking relief, the Hansberrys drove to a park where they enjoyed the cool breeze that blows off Lake Michigan after sunset.

Stretched out on a blanket under a starry sky, Carl Hansberry told his children stories about how the ancient Greeks believed the constellations — Pegasus, Orion, and Andromeda — were formed, but his story about the North Star and the Drinking Gourd, also known as the Big Dipper, interested Lorraine the most. Lying there under the stars, she listened to her father tell stories about how slaves used songs and code words to communicate with one another.

For the old man is waitin'
For to carry you to freedom
If you follow the drinking gourd.
Follow, follow, follow
If you follow the drinking gourd.

"Follow the drinking gourd" was the message that kept runaway slaves moving along the Underground Railroad, a network of routes used by slaves to escape North.

Like so many runaway slaves before him, grandfather George Perry had followed the North Star to freedom. Lorraine wondered what it might have been like being a slave. As hard as she tried, she was never able to comprehend how one human being could own another. The idea of "master" was incomprehensible.

Lorraine visited her maternal grandmother in Tennessee when she was about seven. She remembered very little about the trip, but loved sitting on her grandmother's porch eating cupcakes and listening to stories about her grandfather's escape from slavery. Her experiences there left a lasting impression on the child who would one day be a writer. Lorraine's grandmother died soon after the visit. Years later, Lorraine wrote of her grandmother: ". . . she was born in slavery and had memories of it and they didn't sound anything like *Gone With the Wind. . . .*"

Chicago summers were always hot. Most of the time the adults sat on back porches, fanned with folded newspapers, and talked in quiet tones, while the neighborhood children played another popular game, "May I." The players chose a mama, the authority figure, who stood about twenty or thirty feet away from the players and issued orders, "Take one giant step, or one teeny step." Players had to remember to say "May I?" before obeying the command or they lost a turn and were sent back to the starting point.

Reflecting on the game years later, Lorraine wrote:

It is a long time. One forgets the reason for the game. (For children's games are always explicit in their reasons for being. To play is to win something. Or not to be "it." Or to be high pointer, or outdoer, or something — just the winner. But after a time one forgets.)

Why was it important to take a small step, a teeny step, or the most desired of all — one GIANT step?

A giant step to where?

The questions she asked were not about the game itself. They were a metaphor for questions she was asking about her own life at the time. Where was *she* going? How would *she* get there? Whose permission did she need? And what would happen if she forgot to ask, "May I?"

4

During the 1930s Southern schools were legally segregated. Black children often walked miles to an all-black school, passing several schools in their community that were reserved for white children. In Northern cities, children attended neighborhood schools. Since the neighborhoods were segregated, so were the schools. That is why Lorraine began kindergarten at Betsy Ross Elementary, an all-black school near her home on the South Side. It wasn't an old school — in fact it was new — but it was so poorly built and equipped, it was already showing signs of deterioration. Many years later, Lorraine described it as a:

. . . ghetto school, a school for black children and, therefore, one in which as many things as possible might be safely thought of as "expendable." That, after all, was why it existed: not to give education, but to withhold as much as possible, just as the ghetto itself exists not to give people homes, but to cheat them out of as much decent housing as possible.

Throughout elementary school, young Lorraine was often on the losing end of fights, yet she didn't fear or loathe her classmates, in fact she embraced them and tried to learn from both the poverty that made them so angry, and the prosperity that surrounded her.

Nothing fascinated Lorraine more than the streetwise girls who stood in clusters, used swear words, and picked fights. She longed to know what it would be like to wear a house key around her neck, never realizing that her classmates wore them to let themselves into cold, shabby apartments. Often their parents were divorced or unemployed. Sometimes, in a desperate need to be more like these girls, Lorraine wore a skate key around her neck to pretend she was a latchkey child. But pretend just wasn't the same.

Seeing herself in comparison with many of her classmates, she described herself as:

A serious odd-talking kid, who could neither jump double dutch nor understand their games, but who — classically — envied them. And their costumes. And the things that, somehow, gave them joy: quarters, fights, their fascination to come into the carpeted quiet of our apartment. They, understandably, never understood (or believed) my envy — and they never will.

Lorraine's classmates enjoyed coming home with her, because the Hansberry home was always warm, cheery, and smelled of something good to eat. Carl and Nannie Hansberry were outgoing, gracious people, who were generous and supportive. People often came to them for help, because they were honest and discreet. Carl was known for giving his tenants credit and Nannie was always willing to lend a helping hand to people in need.

Carl and Nannie Hansberry

Without a doubt, Carl was the undisputed head of the family. He was a no-nonsense parent who insisted upon two things: loyalty to the family and to the race. Carl's goals for himself were high and they were no less high for his children. Success was expected. Accomplishments were acknowledged by him, but rarely praised. "Do you praise someone for breathing?" Mamie said matter-of-factly. "Doing well was a part of our daily lives." On this Carl Hansberry made no compromise.

"My father's enduring image in my mind is that of a man whom kings might have imitated," Lorraine wrote in her journal. But while it is easy to look up to a king, it is hard for a little girl to approach a king and give him a surprise hug around the neck. "We were not hugged," Lorraine said, describing her parents' relationship with her as "utilitarian" — they did what they had to do without a lot of emotion.

Big sister Mamie took issue with Lorraine on this point. "I'm sorry people have gotten the impression over the years that our family was cold and unfeeling," said Mamie. "Lorraine was still very young when she wrote a lot of that stuff — especially that part about our parents' relationship to us kids being 'utilitarian.' Let me assure you, there was never a more loved and cared for person than Lorraine Hansberry, and there was never a more adoring father and mother than Carl and Nannie Hansberry!"

Lorraine's writings seem to contradict Mamie, but considering she was only in her early twenties when she made most of her journal entries, Lorraine was probably sorting out some of her feelings and trying to put them into perspective. If she had lived longer, it is possible Lorraine might have regarded her parents in a different way.

Nannie Hansberry was an efficient housewife who ran an orderly house, although she was a busy woman, active in civic, political, and social projects. Meals were served on time, especially breakfast, and all the children were expected to be at the table, properly dressed — no bed clothing was allowed, not even on Saturday.

Very often there were visitors at the dinner table — sometimes a friend of Lorraine's or Mamie's who happened to drop by, or at other times, a prominent African-American social or political leader. The dignitaries who ate across from Lorraine have been the subjects of many books: Walter White, director of the National Association for the Advancement of Colored People (NAACP), W.E.B. DuBois, editor of the NAACP's *Crisis* magazine; Langston Hughes, poet; performers Paul Robeson and Duke Ellington; the 1936 Olympic gold medalist, Jesse Owens, and a wide variety of businessmen and local politicians. All visitors — young or old — were welcomed and treated with kindness and generosity. Just in case there were extra mouths to feed, Mrs. Hansberry usually kept an extra pot of soup on the back burner.

Walter Francis White,
Executive Secretary
of the NAACP

Often dinner table talk covered current events. More than a few guests looked askance when the Hansberry children were invited to participate in the conversation. In an age when children were generally discouraged from "jumping in grown folk's conversation," the Hansberrys invited — and sometimes challenged — their children to participate in discussions. The children were encouraged to have at least some knowledge of current events and be prepared to offer an opinion or express an idea with poise and clarity. At an early age, Lorraine joined in the family debates and talked about concepts with startling confidence. "One won an argument because, if facts gave out," she wrote with humor, "one invented them — with color! The only sinful people in the world were dull people." And the Hansberrys were anything but dull.

The Hansberrys deliberately established a pattern and practice of critical thinking and self-expression for their children. Lorraine was a product of her parents' desire to advance the cause of African-American equality through intelligent and articulate leadership. Lorraine may not have known it, and if she had she probably would have rejected the idea, but she was being reared to be a leader.

ſ

The Hansberrys were die-hard Republicans, as many blacks were at that time. Nannie was a Republican committeewoman for their ward, and Carl was an active member of the party.

One frequent visitor to the Hansberry household was Oscar De-Priest, a black Republican congressman who had been elected to the U.S. House of Representatives in 1928. DePriest was the first black man to be sent to the United States Congress since Reconstruction, and the first ever to be seated from the North. Counted among his supporters were the Hansberrys.

Congressman Oscar DePriest, the first black man elected to the House of Representatives in the twentieth century

DePriest, like Carl and Nannie, had migrated to Chicago from the South and built a successful real estate business. He had been elected to the Cook County Board of Commissioners in 1904 and the Board of Aldermen in 1915. Although he'd been indicted on charges of accepting bribes to provide police protection for gamblers and forced to resign, he was later acquitted of all charges.

When Congressman Martin Madden died in 1928, DePriest had decided to run for the First Illinois Congressional seat. Hansberry had contributed both time and money to the campaign. Despite the scandals that plagued the DePriest campaign, South Side blacks turned out in record numbers to vote for one of their own. He won the three-way election, but several more hurdles stood in his path.

Lorraine had heard DePriest tell the story of how he had been sworn in over the objections of Southern Democrats, who were plotting to keep the newly elected congressman from taking the oath of office. When the Speaker of the House of Representatives, Nicholas Longworth, heard about the floor fight the Southerners were planning, he devised a plan of his own to help DePriest. Congressman William "Bill" Clay, from Missouri, described the maneuver in his book *Just Permanent Interests:*

> *The customary procedure for swearing members into the House was by state delegations in alphabetical order. Southern Congressmen from Alabama, Arkansas, Florida, and Georgia normally would have been seated prior to those from Illinois. Under the rules, anyone already sworn in could offer a motion challenging the seating of any member whose name was presented later. But, Speaker Longworth caught DePriest's enemies off-guard when he announced that all members would stand and be administered the oath of office at the same time. The ploy worked. Simultaneously alongside 434 others, DePriest took his seat as a member of the most prestigious legislative body in the world.*

DePriest instantly became one of the most popular and influential black men in America, but by 1932, black people's loyalty to the party of Abraham Lincoln was waning. The Republican Hoover administration had failed to deal effectively with the ravaging effects of the Depression. It was a rare time when the political interests of poor whites and poor blacks seemed to coincide. Franklin D. Roosevelt, the Democratic candidate for president, was brilliantly portrayed as a friend of the poor and downtrodden, while President Herbert Hoover was portrayed as loyal to the rich and powerful. Democratic promises of economic recovery and drastic changes to help working class people drew blacks and whites away from the Republican party.

Lorraine was just a toddler when President Roosevelt took office, but she grew up listening to political conversations about his administration. She would have heard how after Roosevelt was elected, he took the helm of the troubled nation and tried to steer it into safer waters. Black people were especially pleased with the way he followed through on his promises. Their morale was further lifted when the president included black men and women in the New Deal programs, such as the Civilian Conservation Corps (CCC), which employed more than 200,000 blacks; the Federal Writers' Project, which helped preserve the stories of former slaves; and the Work Projects Administration (WPA), which employed almost a million black people, among them Charles White, a well-known Chicago artist.

Even though Carl Hansberry wasn't a Democrat, he had to admit that Roosevelt also included black men and women among his advisors. The First Lady threw open the doors of the White House to them, dismissing all criticism regarding her integrated guest lists.

To show her daughters the importance of holding on to a dream, Nannie told them about the most famous of the Roosevelt advisors, Mary McLeod Bethune, a distinguished educator and civil rights leader. She had started Bethune-Cookman College in Daytona Beach, Florida, in 1904 with a mere $1.50 and a huge dream. In 1936 Roosevelt appointed her to head the division of Negro Affairs within the National Youth Administration, one of the New Deal programs designed to help students work their way through school.

By the end of Roosevelt's first term, large numbers of African Americans had deserted the Republican Party, especially in Chicago. Black Republican politicians found it increasingly difficult to seek votes from their poor black constituents, who now perceived their party as the party of the white rich. DePriest, who had served three terms in Congress, lost the 1934 election to Arthur L. Mitchell, a former Republican who had switched to the Democratic Party. The Hansberrys were committed to the struggle against racism and discrimination in America. They were equally as convinced that the Republican party offered blacks more opportunities to achieve that goal. So the Hansberrys remained loyal Republicans.

In addition to their political involvement, the Hansberrys were active members of the NAACP. The year Lorraine was born, the NAACP had launched a successful campaign against the confirmation of Judge John J. Parker as a Supreme Court justice. The North Carolinian had made the comment that the "participation of the Negro in politics [was] a source of evil and danger to both races." And, in 1933, the NAACP represented black educators in the *Gibbs v. Board of Education* case of Montgomery County, Maryland, and won. The state court's decision helped set a precedent for equal pay for black and white teachers.

Lorraine grew up listening to NAACP lawyers planning legal strategies in her living room. During the Roosevelt administration, more liberal judges were appointed to the Supreme Court, so the NAACP took this as a signal to step up its attack on segregation. Case by case, they were able to win more landmark civil rights decisions than ever before, including *Hansberry v. Lee.*

G

During the Depression 40,000 blacks had migrated to Chicago, swelling the population in the Black Belt to more than 250,000. There was a pressing need for more and better housing. As a real estate broker, Carl Hansberry was one of the first to recognize those housing needs and to articulate the immediate dangers of the substandard buildings poor people were forced to occupy. For this, he blamed white brokers who benefited from discriminatory practices in the real estate industry. There was no place for the South Side to expand, because blacks were locked out of all-white communities thanks to the "racially restrictive covenants" many white property owners had recorded and attached to their deeds.

These covenants were contracts in which the property owners in a given area agreed not to allow people of other races to buy, rent, lease, or otherwise occupy homes or apartments that they owned. Typically African Americans and Jews were the targets of these agreements. Although racially restrictive covenants were later declared un-constitutional, these covenants were legal at that time.

Race covenants in the neighborhoods bordering the South Side created great hardships for the growing black community. The Black Belt was boxed in and unable to expand geographically, even though the increased population desperately needed additional housing. What resulted was a much more densely populated area in which the strains of overcrowding were affecting the quality of life for everyone.

In 1937 Carl Hansberry and a team of NAACP lawyers found a loophole that gave them a legal means to strike at housing discrimi-nation indirectly.

Hansberry, with the help of Harry H. Pace, president of the Supreme Liberty Life Insurance Company, and several white realtors, secretly bought two pieces of property at 413 East Sixtieth Street and 6140 Rhodes Avenue, both located in an all-white neighborhood that

An NAACP Legal Defense Fund meeting

was supposedly protected by a racially restrictive covenant. Hansberry and Pace kept their identities secret until the purchase was completed. Pace moved into the property on Sixtieth and the Hansberrys occupied the Rhodes property on May 26, 1937.

Upon discovery of the purchase, a woman named Anna M. Lee filed a class action suit on behalf of the Woodlawn Property Owners' Association and 500 other white property owners to block Pace and Hansberry from living at the two residences.

Lorraine was too young to understand the impact her father's actions would have on their family or the important role her father was playing in the struggle for freedom and justice in America. To understand the importance of *Hansberry v. Lee*, it is necessary to start with a prior case, *Burke v. Kleiman* (1933), which involved the same covenant. In that case, Isaac and Sam Kleiman violated the Woodlawn Property Owners' Association covenant by renting property to a black man named Hall. Olive Ida Burke filed a "representative" or "class action" suit on behalf of herself and 500 other property owners. She claimed that 95% of the property owners had signed an agreement not to permit African Americans to buy, rent, or lease property in the area.

Burke argued that (1) the covenant was legal, (2) the Kleimans knew of the agreement, and (3) that the Kleimans had violated the agreement by renting to Hall. In the course of that trial, the attorneys for both Burke and the Kleimans told the court that the required 95% of the owners had signed the agreement and that the covenant had been duly recorded on February 1, 1928. Based on those statements the judge determined that the covenant was valid. He ordered the Kleimans to stop renting to blacks, and forced Hall, the black tenant, to move out.

In the course of preparing for the *Hansberry v. Lee* trial, the NAACP lawyers discovered through a careful search of the records that only 54% of the white residents of the Woodlawn Property Owners' Association had signed the agreement. They argued that the agreement never took effect; therefore, the residents were free to sell to whomever they wished.

Even though the NAACP's information was correct, Lee's attorneys asserted that, as a matter of law, the court had already determined in *Burke v. Kleiman* that the covenant was legal. Relying on the legal principle of *res judicata* (a Latin term meaning "the matter has been decided"), they countered that for the purposes of law, the covenant was in effect, lawful, and binding on all of the 500 property owners who had been represented in the *Burke* case. It was not lawful to litigate the matter again.

The Circuit Court of Cook County accepted Lee's argument that the entire issue had been disposed of in the *Burke* case and ordered Pace and Hansberry to move out of their homes. They appealed the case.

While Hansberry was in Springfield, Illinois, taking the necessary steps to defend his rights as a property owner, his family was under attack. Mamie was outside watching eight-year-old Lorraine play on the sidewalk when a mob of whites gathered. They yelled racial slurs and made threats. Mrs. Hansberry called her daughters inside. The mob grew angrier. Suddenly a brick was hurled through the window, narrowly missing Lorraine's head. "If it had hit her, it could have been fatal," said Mamie, remembering the incident. During that terrible night her mother and a family friend stayed up, walking from room to room, watching and wondering what might happen next. It wasn't until the family friend went out on the porch and stood there with a shotgun in his hand that the crowd disbanded. Lorraine never forgot that night.

Meanwhile, Hansberry's efforts to have the decision reversed by the Illinois Court of Appeals and the Illinois Supreme Court had proved unsuccessful. Both of these courts ruled that the doctrine of *res judicata* applied and that the parties were bound by the decision of the *Burke* case. Determined to see it through to the full extent of the law, Hansberry's lawyers appealed the case to the highest court in the land, the Supreme Court of the United States. The case attracted nationwide attention, especially in the real estate business and in African-American newspapers.

After announcing that it would hear the case, the Supreme Court noted that it would review the decision of the *Burke* case because of its impact on issues in the Hansberry case. After hearing the arguments from both sides, the court ruled in favor of Hansberry.

The court's decision had a tremendous impact on constitutional law throughout the country, because the court found the "class action" procedure followed in the *Burke* case flawed since the people who were represented were not given any notice and there were no safeguards to assure that their interests were properly represented. The decision in *Burke* was no longer binding on the other property owners. Hansberry and Pace could keep the property.

Hansberry v. Lee didn't put an end to "racially restrictive covenants." That would come later. Still the decision was considered a victory in the black community, because it tore a large breach in the covenant barrier, making it possible for others to attack covenants in similar cases elsewhere. For Hansberry the decision made it possible for the South Side to expand into an area that had been formerly closed to black people. And, for many white property owners who wanted to sell or rent to African Americans, the case enabled them to do so without risk of being sued.

After the case, Hansberry became a hero. He decided to ride the wave of that popularity to Washington and ran for Congress on the Republican ticket in 1940. Actually there were no black Republicans willing to challenge the incumbent in a year when President Roosevelt was running for his third term. The Republican Party wrote off Chicago, which had become a Democratic stronghold, and refused to support Hansberry. By then ten-year-old Lorraine was old enough to participate in her family's political efforts. She helped with her father's campaign by stuffing envelopes, participating in fund-raisers, and accompanying her parents in door-to-door canvassing. Despite their hard work, Carl Hansberry was soundly defeated in the November elections.

Hansberry lost more than the bid for the house seat. During the court battle and the campaign, he had neglected his business and his health, both of which were in serious trouble. A lot of his rental property had deteriorated, which undermined his financial stability.

"Daddy was hurt," remembered Mamie. "But we never realized how much until it was too late." There is no way to know the amount of personal stress Lorraine felt during the strain of these events. But it is certain that the drama of those times was the foundation upon which she developed her most famous work, *A Raisin in the Sun.*

7

On December 7, 1941, Japanese aircraft attacked Pearl Harbor naval base in Hawaii, and the United States entered World War II. The war years helped to shape Lorraine's attitudes as much as her parents' civil rights involvement had. With family and friends in the military, Lorraine spent a lot of time writing letters and worrying about their safety.

While the war in Europe and the Pacific raged, the Hansberrys continued to battle against social and economic injustice on the homefront. In June 1942 a group of white and black Chicagoans organized the Congress on Racial Equality (CORE) with the purpose of conducting nonviolent protests against job discrimination. Carl and Nannie Hansberry were charter members who helped plan action against businesses that didn't hire qualified blacks.

Employment opportunities for blacks had increased a little during the war because of Roosevelt's executive order #8802, which had been issued on June 25, 1941. It forbade racial and religious discrimination in defense industries and government training programs. Still discrimination continued, and a majority of black people remained unemployed. Nicholas Lemann, author of *The Promised Land,* described the employment situation on Chicago's South Side as limited and repressive:

There were no black drivers of yellow cabs, no black sales clerks at the big

department stores in the Loop, no black linemen at Illinois Bell, no black
bus drivers, no black policemen or firemen except at the stations in the
black belt, and no blacks in the building-trades unions.

On a more personal level, Lorraine saw the result of wartime controls. Black Belt rents were frozen at their already high levels. It was common knowledge that African Americans paid more rent for less space and earned lower wages for more work. White realtors enticed whites to move with threats that their property was going to decrease in value. Then they turned around and rented the property to blacks at twice the rate.

Professional blacks had moved to other areas by then, leaving the South Side to deteriorate into a full-fledged ghetto. Run-down kitchenette apartments and decaying three-story tenements lined State Street between 22nd and 51st Streets. Most of the buildings were owned by whites, but a few black realtors, including Hansberry, continued to manage property on the South Side.

Unfortunately, Hansberry had fallen completely out of favor with the powerful Chicago political machine, which was controlled mostly by white Democrats. Suddenly, he began having problems with his rental property. He was cited for more than 150 code violations and wasn't granted extra time to bring the buildings up to standard. He spent a lot of time in court fighting what he believed were unfair citations. Meanwhile, he was repeatedly denied occupancy permits and some of his property was even condemned.

Hansberry's lawyers accused the city government of being vindictive and spiteful, but Hansberry was portrayed as a shameless slumlord who profited from renting substandard property to his own people. "That broke our father's heart, because he had fought so long and hard to improve housing conditions for blacks," remembered Mamie. "This personal attack on his character was the beginning of the end for him. I was old enough to know. Our mother never talked about Daddy's business problems in front of Lorraine. She was in grade school and mother felt there wasn't a need to clutter her life with their problems."

The question of whether Hansberry was a slumlord continues to be debated even now. In his own defense, Hansberry said he was being punished unfairly. There were other property owners whose apartments were in far worse shape than his, yct they hadn't been fined or their property condemned. This may have been true, but his argument wasn't convincing to some community leaders. They countered that since he was an African-American property owner, he should set a standard higher than others and thereby establish a level for others to match.

According to Mamie, Hansberry yielded to the criticism and voluntarily improved several rental units, but "when he raised the rents to compensate for the repairs, he was attacked for that, too. People don't realize how politically motivated it was back then," she says in retrospect. "If Lorraine were alive, she'd tell you the same thing. There's another side to this story that a lot of people don't want to talk about. They never mention how some of our tenants moved into our apartments, literally tore them up, never paid rent, and moved out in the middle of the night. Daddy lost more money than he ever earned."

The truth of the matter is probably somewhere between the two extremes. More than likely Carl Hansberry was outside the political umbrella and was therefore an easy target. But it is also true that many of his rental units were in bad condition. It is difficult to burn a stick at both ends. Hansberry set himself up for attack when he demanded better housing for blacks on one hand, while on the other hand, his own property, for whatever reasons, was substandard. Whenever Lorraine, like Mamie, was asked about her father's enterprises, she became defensive and very protective of his character.

The family's stress mounted when Lorraine's brother Perry opposed the draft because he felt a democracy that condoned segregated fighting forces was morally corrupt. He was convinced that he shouldn't be forced to defend a country that neither respected his rights as a citizen nor granted him the protections guaranteed by the

United States Constitution. Carl Hansberry was looking at his own militancy in his son. He knew that Perry and other young black men felt no differently than his generation had during World War I. Carl no doubt remembered what W.E.B. DuBois had written in *Crisis* magazine regarding black soldiers returning from World War I. In part, DuBois had written:

> *This is the country to which we Soldiers of Democracy return. This is the fatherland for which we fought! But it is our fatherland. It was right for us to fight. The faults of our country are our faults, under similar circumstances, we would fight again. But by the God of Heaven, we are cowards and jackasses if now that war is over, we do not marshal every ounce of our brain and brawn to fight a sterner, longer, more unbending battle against the forces of hell in our own land.*
>   *We return.*
>   *We return from fighting.*
>   *We return fighting.*
>   *Make way for Democracy! We saved it in France, and by the Great Jehovah, we will save it in the United States of America, or know the reason why.*

Carl, Sr., agreed with his son, in principle, but suggested that he fight the system using legal means. Carl didn't think his son had a chance of winning or changing anything taking the course of action he had planned. Perry disagreed with his father.

"When Perry and Daddy disagreed it was like two titans clashing," Mamie said. "Lorraine would rush to her room and close the door, because she couldn't stand to see two people she loved so angry with each other." In the end, Perry relented and served in the army. So did Carl, Jr.

Meanwhile, Lorraine finished grade school in 1944 and was in high school the year the United States dropped atomic bombs on Hiroshima and Nagasaki. Appalled by the death toll, she wrote poems and stories about beautiful things such as clouds, flowers, and music. Mamie, on vacation from Howard University, and Nannie discovered some of Lorraine's writing. They both were shocked at how good some of it was. Like a lot of fledgling writers, Lorraine was apprehensive about sharing her work, but with a little encouragement, she gained more confidence. Soon, she was writing letters to government officials stating her opinions about issues she felt were important, like peace and equal rights. As a freshman at Englewood High School she wrote a story about football and won a school prize.

Lorraine was a shy and overweight teenager. "Oh, yes, she was short and plump — a little too plump for Mother," Mamie said. "Mother believed that if Lorraine didn't look good, she wouldn't feel good about herself. I happen to think Mother was right."

Lorraine didn't think so. She resented her mother's criticism and accused her of being vain ". . . the product of robust semi-feudal backwardness."

Mamie objected. "Mother was a feminine woman, sure! But she was strong. Who was it that took charge and ran things when Daddy was involved in his many projects? Mother. Who was it that stood toe to toe with a gang of racists who threatened her children? Our mother."

Nannie Hansberry wanted her daughters to know that they were brilliant and beautiful. Mamie elaborated, "Let me tell you something, before the 1960s, before the slogan 'black is beautiful' became popular, those two words — brilliant and beautiful — were rarely spoken about black women. Rightly or wrongly, Mother was trying to pad us girls for the hurts the world was going to heap on our heads."

Although the mother-daughter generational conflict resolved itself as Lorraine grew older, Lorraine's resistance to what she called her mother's "intense femininity" lasted far beyond her teenage years.

Life in the Hansberrys' house wasn't too different from that of any other middle-class family, but in 1945 things began to change. Lorraine's father had been treated for high blood pressure for years. His condition had worsened, and by the end of the year, he felt, as many blacks had before him, that African Americans would never find peace or justice in the United States. Over the years he had become friends with several Mexican businessmen who had visited the family in Chicago. They convinced the Hansberrys to buy a home in Palanco, a suburb outside Mexico City, and relocate there.

Leaving his older children in charge of the real estate business, Carl moved to Mexico. Nannie and Lorraine followed in a few weeks. The family had high hopes that life there would be better, and for a few months, Carl's health seemed to improve. Then, while Nannie and Lorraine were back in Chicago making plans for the final move, Carl suddenly died on March 7, 1946, at the age of 51. It was just short of Lorraine's sixteenth birthday.

Although Carl Hansberry's death certificate listed the cause of death as cerebral hemorrhage, in a letter to the editor of *The New York Times*, dated April 23, 1964, Lorraine named racism as the cause:

> *My father was typical of a generation of Negroes who believed that the "American Way" could successfully be made to work to democratize the United States. Thus, twenty-five years ago, he spent a small personal fortune, his considerable talents, and many good years of his life fighting, in association with NAACP attorneys, Chicago's "restrictive covenants" in one of the nation's ugliest ghettoes . . . The cost, in emotional turmoil, time and money, led to my father's early death as a permanently embittered exile in a foreign country when he saw that after such sacrificial efforts the Negroes of Chicago were as ghetto-locked as ever . . .*

Lorraine and her mother stayed in Chicago, and Mamie, Perry, and Carl, Jr., who were all married with families of their own, continued to manage their father's business. Lorraine accepted her father's death in a practical sense, but he remained ever-present in her life. It is interesting to note that in her major works the father is always dead, but very much a part of the family's ongoing decision making and problem solving.

8

Lorraine had been attending Englewood High School since January 1944. The Hansberrys had bought a home in Englewood, previously an all-white section of the South Side, but by the time of their move, a neighborhood in transition. As soon as blacks moved in, whites began moving out, and naturally anger and frustration, expressed at home, spilled over into the schools. Aside from her own childhood experiences, Lorraine knew that Chicago had a long and ugly history regarding race relations.

Although the Englewood High School administration tried to ease the relations between black and white students, trouble was always bubbling just below the surface. On the wave of this citywide tension, a few white students at Englewood staged a demonstration — a strike — the purpose of which has long been forgotten. Lorraine and the other "well dressed" black students from respectable homes huddled together, feeling angry but helpless.

"Then had come the veterans," Lorraine wrote, describing the incident years later. "Volunteers from Wendell Phillips . . . and DuSable." These were black high schools located in the predominately black areas on the South Side. Carloads of students had come, carrying baseball bats and ready to do battle with the protesters.

The word had gone into the ghetto: the ofays are out on strike and beating up and raping colored girls under the viaduct out South! *And the summary, traditional and terse: WE BETTER GO 'CAUSE THEM LITTLE CHICKEN-SHIT NIGGERS OUT THERE AIN'T ABOUT TO FIGHT!*

And so they had come, pouring out of the bowels of the ghetto, the children of the unqualified oppressed: the black working-class in their costumes of pegged pants and conked heads and tight skirts and almost knee-length sweaters and — worst of all — colored anklets, held up with rubber bands!

Yes, they had come and they had fought. It had taken the Mayor and the visit of a famous movie star to get everyone's mind back on other things again. He had been terribly handsome and full of speeches on "tolerance" and had also given a lot of autographs. But she had been unimpressed.

She never would forget one thing: They had fought back!

Lorraine was completely taken by the black girls from the ghetto. They were unlike the middle-class girls at Englewood and did not care what white students thought about their clothing, their hairstyles, or their speech and manner. The boys from the ghetto did not worry how their actions would reflect on their families' position in society. The ghetto blacks had come to meet their attackers without pause, ready to fight.

Lorraine had been taught to overcome adversity by being a better thinker than her opponent and to resolve problems through reason and law. But there was also an angry part of herself that wanted to throw reason and responsibility to the winds and go into pitched battle against any form of injustice. This incident pushed Lorraine a little closer to the revolutionary thinker she would one day become.

9

Since elementary school, Lorraine had decided her heroes were Toussaint L'Ouverture, the liberator of Haiti, and Hannibal, the African general. Her favorite writer was Pearl Buck, the author of *The Good Earth*. Since her freshman year in high school, Lorraine had been allowed to go out on well-chaperoned dates to school dances and plays. On one date she'd seen her first play, *Dark of the Moon*, written by Howard Richardson and William Berney. She had been mesmerized by the "folk musical" and listened to every word. After that night she was convinced that she wanted to write a play, but first she had the problem of passing her English class.

Lorraine was introduced to Shakespeare and other literary greats by an English teacher, believed to be Miss Kathleen Rigby. Dubbed "Pale Hecate," the classical Greek goddess of the moon and witchcraft, Miss Rigby worked a special kind of magic on her young students, especially Lorraine.

One day, quite unexpectedly, Pale Hecate gave Lorraine's paper back with a big red "C" sprawled across the page and announced with a shriek, "Cheat!"

Lorraine started to say *she hadn't done anything*... but before she could finish, Pale Hecate interrupted, stating "... that is precisely the point." Lorraine believed the "C" was for average work. But the teacher had her own definition: "For them that would do half when all is called for; for them that will slip and slide through life at the edge of their minds, never once pushing into the interior to see what wonders are hiding there — content to drift along on whatever gets them by, cheating themselves, cheating the world, cheating Nature! That is what the 'C' means, my dear child."

Lorraine wasn't impressed with many of her teachers, but she liked Pale Hecate and years later, credited Pale Hecate with being the source of her love of drama.

Lorraine's passion for the theater, Shakespeare, and writing were matched only by her love of Africa. Many blacks during the 1940s and '50s were confused about the land, the people, and their history. They had mistaken ideas that Africa was a "dark continent," inhabited by cannibals and tigers, neither of which is found in Africa. For centuries, African Americans were taught to be ashamed of their African ancestry. In history textbooks, their story began on a crowded slave ship. Hollywood created stereotypical images of Africans as spear-throwing savages, running around half naked with bones in their noses. No wonder one of the most painful racial slurs was "Go back to Africa!"

Lorraine knew better, because her father had provided books written by W.E.B. DuBois; Carter G. Woodson, the historian and writer who started the celebration that is now black history month in

1926; and of course, her uncle, Professor William Leo Hansberry. Their writings had given her a more accurate and positive introduction to African studies.

Correspondence with and visits from her famous uncle helped Lorraine during the difficult years after her father's death. Although Professor Hansberry was a well-respected teacher, scholar, and Africanist, to Lorraine he was just "Uncle Leo," Daddy's brother, the one who sent postcards and letters from faraway places with interesting stamps. When he wasn't in Africa studying and researching, Leo Hansberry was lecturing, writing papers, and teaching at Howard University in Washington, D.C.

Like Lorraine's father, Leo Hansberry was no stranger to adversity. He'd earned his B.A. (1921) and M.A. (1932) degrees from Harvard University in anthropology and archaeology. The basis of his work was to show that "Africa rather than Asia was in all probability the birthplace of the human race," and that "it was they [Africans], it appears, who first learned and then taught the rest of mankind how to make and use tools, to develop a religion, to practice art, to domesticate animals, to smelt metals — particularly iron, and to create and maintain a deliberately constructed and tradition-bound state."

William Leo Hansberry, the noted scholar and Africanist

Building on the historical works of DuBois and Carter G. Woodson, Professor Hansberry added his own assertions drawn from his archaeological study. Within some circles his ideas were dismissed as unbelievable and challenged for lack of supporting evidence. When Professor Hansberry submitted a research proposal to the Rosenwald and Carnegie foundations, his major adviser at Harvard, Professor Earnest A. Hooton, chairman of the anthropology department, wrote:

I am quite confident that no present-day scholar has anything like the knowledge of this field (pre-history of Africa) that Hansberry has developed. He has been unable to take the Ph.D. degree, because there is no university or institution that has manifested a really profound interest in this subject . . .   .

Unfortunately, he was still denied the grant, but Hooton's support helped establish Hansberry's credibility and his work was recognized by some scholars. He was eventually awarded several grants.

"Lorraine was like a sponge, soaking up all Uncle Leo had to offer," said Mamie. "The things she learned from him weren't in any textbooks at the time. She was getting information then that is just now getting into books."

But during the postwar era, African Americans began questioning the exclusion of African and African-American history and literature in textbooks. They sought a more accurate representation of their story, and soon Professor Hansberry was in demand as a speaker and teacher. While some of Lorraine's classmates thought Timbuktu was the name of a mythical place located faraway and hard to find, Lorraine knew that Timbuktu, Jenne, and Gao were large trading centers located in the West African kingdoms of Ghana, Mali, and Songhay. Lorraine expressed her own knowledge of Africa in this excerpt from her journal:

. . . she had spent hours of her younger years poring over maps of the African continent, postulating and fantasizing: Ibo, Mandingo, Hausa, Yoruba, Ashanti, Dahomean. *Who, who were they! In her emotions she was sprung from the Southern Zulu and the Central Pygmy, the*

Eastern Watusi and the treacherous slave-trading Western Ashanti them-
selves. She was Kikuyu and Masai, ancient cousins of hers had made the
exquisite forged sculpture of Benin, while surely even more ancient rela-
tives sat upon the throne at Abu Simbel watching over the Nile.

Learning about ancient Africa was interesting and exciting, but Lorraine also wanted to know about modern-day Africa, too.

Europe had dominated the second largest continent since the
nineteenth century, but after the establishment of the United Nations
following World War II, Africans began petitioning the world to help
them end colonialism. Lorraine saw these struggles as parallel to the
American fight for independence. Why then, she wondered, didn't
American diplomats speak out against the colonial powers that had
robbed Africa of its people, land, and resources? With or without
America's help, she concluded, the "Free Africa" movement was an
ever-strengthening eddy, and at the forefront of that movement was
Leo Hansberry. Even then, Lorraine wanted to be a part of that struggle for freedom, too.

Everybody noticed, except Lorraine herself, that at seventeen she
had grown into a lovely young woman, witty, intelligent, sensitive,
twenty pounds slimmer, and full of energy. She graduated with average grades, above average potential, and either because of, or in spite
of, Pale Hecate, a love of Shakespeare. There was no way then to measure the full extent of the education she'd received growing up the
daughter of Carl and Nannie Hansberry. The ratio of black students
to whites at Englewood had increased since her family had moved
into the neighborhood. Now there were 118 blacks in her January
1948 graduating class of 169. She'd been elected gym secretary and
president of the debate club. She remembered her graduation as not
especially a happy or sad event. She missed her father very much, but
managed not to cry.

10

While Mamie openly enjoyed all aspects of her family's wealth and social status, Lorraine rejected the prestige, although she took full advantage of the opportunities her family's money made possible, especially with regard to her education. She didn't apply to an all-black university, because she didn't want to go South, and she didn't want to take part in the social scene she'd been avoiding most of her life. She applied to and was accepted at the University of Wisconsin.

A few weeks after Lorraine's high-school graduation, Mamie helped her choose her college wardrobe and pack, and after a tearful good-bye, Mamie and Perry drove Lorraine to the university, a hundred miles away in Madison. It snowed on the way so the campus looked like a crystal fantasy when they arrived. Since there were no dormitory rooms available, Mamie made arrangements to move Lorraine into Langdon Manor, a large, two-story residence for girls, which until then had been all white.

Lorraine quickly adjusted to her new environment and took delight in being on her own — away from her mother, Mamie, and her

Lorraine (third row) and her housemates at the University of Wisconsin

brothers. She made friends quickly and spent hours talking about boys, sex, politics, God, books, music, and art, but she found the traditional course offerings uninspired and boring.

The only thing that hadn't managed to disappoint her about college was the snow, until one day, quite by accident, she wandered into a production of Sean O'Casey's *Juno and the Paycock,* heralded by some as one of the most powerful plays written in the twentieth century. Set during the Irish Civil War in 1922, the action centers around Juno Boyle's attempt to overcome poverty, her husband's drunkenness, and the collapse of her family. O'Casey, who had been born in a Dublin slum, presented characters who were uniquely Irish, yet universal in their appeal.

"I love Sean O'Casey," Lorraine wrote. "O'Casey never fools you about the Irish, you see . . . the Irish drunkard, the Irish braggart, the Irish liar . . . and the genuine heroism which must naturally emerge when you tell the truth about people. This, to me, is the height of artistic perception and is the most rewarding kind of thing that can happen in drama."

Lorraine was so impressed with O'Casey's vitality and uncompromising social conscience that she decided drama was her calling. She took a course in set design but the professor gave her a D, because, according to one Hansberry biographer, "He did not want to encourage a young black woman in a field dominated by whites, or so he said." But that wasn't enough to stop Lorraine from pursuing her dream.

Lorraine completed her first semester at the University of Wisconsin with fair grades and a pack-a-day smoking habit. She spent the summer reading and writing, mostly letters. Mamie, Perry, and Carl, Jr., were successfully running the family business, but their problems with corrupt city officials continued. Although Lorraine was invited to join the family business, property management didn't hold the same fascination for her as it had for her father. But, she did embrace politics with the traditional Hansberry enthusiasm.

Back at Wisconsin in the fall of '48, Lorraine decided to support the third party presidential candidate, Henry Wallace of the Progressive Party, and she was even elected the campus chairman of the

Sean O'Casey was one of Lorraine's favorite playwrights.

Young Progressives of America.

The Progressive Party was started in 1912 by former President Theodore Roosevelt, the result of a split within the Republican Party. Comprised of mostly middle-class and urban workers, the Progressives had a reputation for wanting more government involvement and advocated social and industrial reform. Their position on civil rights called for an end to racial segregation and equal opportunity for people regardless of race, sex, or religion. In 1948 those were considered radical ideas, but they were appealing ideas to Lorraine.

Henry Wallace had been elected vice president during Franklin

Lorraine supported Henry Wallace in his bid for the presidency.

D. Roosevelt's third term. Born in Iowa in 1888, Wallace was a successful farmer and the editor of several farming magazines. Before choosing Wallace as his running mate, Roosevelt had appointed him Secretary of Agriculture during his first two terms.

Still Wallace ran a miserable third behind Republican candidate Thomas Dewey and the Democratic winner, Harry Truman. Afterward Lorraine's interest in political parties waned, but not her interest in social justice. Several of Hansberry's biographers believe it was her involvement with these young radicals that "probably fanned the slow fire of the young revolutionary."

For the time being she returned to her art, especially the theater. "I was intrigued by the theater. Mine was the same old story," she wrote, "sort of hanging around little acting groups, developing a feeling that the theater embraces everything I like all at one time."

11

Lorraine spent the summer of 1949 studying painting at the University of Guadalajara art workshop in Ajijic, Mexico. She studied the murals of Diego Rivera (1886–1957), the bold paintings of José Clemente Orozco (1883–1949), and other North and South American artists.

Once again the formal learning experience bored her, and she escaped the academic setting whenever she could to explore firsthand the sounds and colors of everyday Mexican life. Moving freely among the people — especially in the marketplaces — and using her textbook Spanish to communicate, allowed her to learn in a more practical way.

On her own she discovered that for centuries Mexico's mountains had separated its people, so their use of colors and patterns differed from region to region. She was even more interested in the similarities between Mexican and African pottery and handicrafts and fascinated by the common patterns of their basketry and beadwork.

Lorraine was reading everything she could about Africa, especially about the struggle for freedom from the colonial powers. Lorraine had learned a new and exciting term, *decolonization*. It meant the transfer of power from the controlling colonial countries, such as England, France, or Belgium, to new, independent nations in Africa, the Middle East, Asia, and the Caribbean. Between 1945 and 1947 decolonization had begun spreading in Asia and the Middle East. Many colonized African countries also began to push for their independence. But by 1948 the trend had slowed, and decolonization would be slower in Africa. Yet the people there were no longer willing to wait for colonial governments to "give" them their countries back; many of them decided to fight for their freedom. Jomo Kenyatta was one of those people.

Lorraine read Kenyatta's *Facing Mount Kenya* so many times, she could quote whole pages from memory. The last page clearly and con-cisely stated Kenyatta's spirited commitment to freeing his country from English domination:

> *The African is conditioned, by the cultural and social institutions of cen-turies, to a freedom of which Europe had little conception, and it is not in his nature to accept serfdom forever. He realises that he must fight un-ceasingly for his own complete emancipation . . .*

Back on campus, Lorraine shifted her social and political inter-ests toward Africa. Her knowledge of Africa, while impressive, was idealized. After meeting and becoming familiar with Africans on cam-pus, she realized that she was guilty of romanticizing the whole idea of revolution. Sensitive to this issue, she wrote a semi-autobiographical play about Candace, a college student caught up in the drama of African independence and a "gorgeous black knight-without-armor" named Monasse.

Candace tries to seduce Monasse, but in this scene she prods him for information about the liberation movements that were underway in his homeland.

CANDACE
(*wistfully*)

I wish I were an African . . .

MONASSE
(*nodding*)

So you could be — a revolutionary?

CANDACE

Millions of Africans marching, singing, carrying their leaders on
their shoulders —

MONASSE

You've seen only thousands at the most so far; and the shoulders
of other men is not a very good place for leaders . . .

CANDACE

Why are you always like that?

MONASSE

Like what?

CANDACE

Well, so disparaging about all the *big* things.

MONASSE

(*Meeting her eyes intently*)

Because you are serious enough about them for both of us, I
think.

THEY *freeze.*

Six "serious" hours later she arrives back at the dorm filled to
bursting and savoring every detail she plans to share with her
roommate, Mariela. She was sure of it now: he hadn't *said* it but
the look was unmistakable in his eyes: *Monasse had his ties with the
Liberation!* And, moreover, right in the middle of page 238 of *Facing Mount Kenya,* he had closed the book and kissed her. "That
ought to hold good ole' Mariela!"

The manuscript was never finished and remains unpublished.
She would incorporate elements of this story in several of her later
works.

In the winter of 1950, Lorraine heard Frank Lloyd Wright
(1867–1959), the pioneer architect whose projects ranged from vases
to buildings, speak at the university's brand-new student union. She
remembered Wright's visit well and wrote about it years later.

*Addressing the packed hall, [Wright] attacked almost everything — and, fore-
most among them, the building he was standing in for its violation of the or-*

ganic principles of architecture; he attacked babbitry and the nature of educa-
tion. Lorraine agreed with Wright's assertion that, "we put in so many fine
plums and get out so many fine prunes." Everyone laughed — the faculty ner-
vously I guess; but the students cheered. Lorraine left the university in Febru-
ary 1950 to pursue, as she described it, "an education of another kind."

After studying art at Roosevelt University in Chicago during that
summer, Lorraine announced that she was going to New York. Nannie
tried to convince her that the proper thing to do was marry an eligible
young man from one of Chicago's fine black families and settle down.
When Lorraine insisted that she wasn't ready to get married, Nannie
reminded her "head-strong daughter" that she was a "nice girl" and
living alone in New York City was not the proper thing for her to do.
Lorraine assured her mother that she was capable of taking care of
herself, and besides, there were more writing opportunities open to
her in New York. Rather than force the issue, Nannie gave her "permission," although she knew Lorraine was going with or without her
blessing. By late fall 1950 Lorraine boarded a train bound for the Big
Apple.

Roosevelt University, where Lorraine Hansberry studied art

CHAPTER II

BLACK . . .

Language symbols, spoken and written, have permitted Man to abstract his awareness of the world and transmit his feelings about it to his fellows . . . That may be the most extraordinary accomplishment in the universe for all we know. And even if it is not, it is certainly one of the most wondrous and marvelous things to have happened in this particular world of ours.

And it is certainly too important a gift to waste in not using it, to the best of one's ability, in behalf of the human race.

An excerpt from "The Nation Needs Your Gifts," by
LORRAINE HANSBERRY

12

1950.

The Korean War. The infamous McCarthy Era.

Major newspaper headlines announced: U. S. BACKS SOUTH KOREA AGAINST NORTH. When North Korean communists invaded South Korea in June 1950, United States troops were sent to support South Korean soldiers who were poorly trained and no match against the Soviet-armed North Koreans.

The threat of communism rapidly became Americans' primary concern, but fear reached hysterical levels when Senator Joseph McCarthy from Wisconsin initiated a communist witch-hunt that destroyed thousands of lives through coercion and innuendo.

Speaking to the Republican Women's Club in Wheeling, West Virginia, McCarthy held up a paper, claiming that it contained the names of 205 people who were "known to the Secretary of State, [Dean Acheson] as being members of the Communist Party" and who

Senator Joseph McCarthy claimed that the U.S. government was infiltrated by communists.

nevertheless were still "working and shaping policy in the State Department." Although a Senate committee said McCarthy's charges were "a big lie," McCarthy persisted in his attack against those he called "twisted-thinking New Dealers."

1950.

African Americans were also in the news. In January more than 4,000 delegates from 100 national organizations met in Washington, D.C., to protest the treatment of blacks in America, especially soldiers who continued to fight in segregated units.

At mid-year, poet Gwendolyn Brooks became the first African American to win the Pulitzer Prize, for her second volume of poems, *Annie Allen,* and twenty-two-year-old Althea Gibson was the first black woman to be accepted by the United States Lawn Tennis Association.

It was announced in September that Dr. Ralph Bunche, career diplomat with the United Nations, had received the Nobel Peace Prize for his work as a United Nations peace negotiator. The Korean War dominated the news all year, but in the fall African Americans mourned the heavy loss of black soldiers in a sixteen-hour battle in the taking of Yechon.

In November no headlines proclaimed the arrival of Lorraine Hansberry to New York. She was just one of the thousands of talented people who flocked to the city during the 1950s, filled with hopes and dreams. "We thought Lorraine would stay in New York for a few months, get lonely, then come home," said Mamie. But everybody back home was surprised by Lorraine's tenacity.

Within a few weeks she'd found both a job typing, which paid an average salary of $31.70 a week, and a four-room apartment on the Lower East Side that she shared with three other women. To earn extra money and gain writing experience, she wrote articles for the Young Progressives of America, an organization she had joined in college.

Harlem inspired many of her articles. Historically, blacks began moving into Harlem in the early 1900s, but by 1950 only a glimmer of the grandeur that had once been associated with it remained. In its heyday between 1915 and 1930, Harlem was the center of African-American culture and politics. A popular slang expression from that time was, "If you wanted to be in the know, Harlem is where you need to go." Blacks from all over the country looked to Harlem as the un-official capital of African-American art, literature, music, dance, and leadership. It was home of the swanky Cotton Club, the jumpin' Savoy, the elite Dark Tower, and the fashionable Paul Laurence Dunbar Apartments where the poet Countee Cullen, W.E.B. DuBois, and the first African-American general in the United States Army, Brigadier General Benjamin O. Davis, Sr., used to live. In fact, visiting Harlem in the 1950s was a tour of what "used to be." Old Harlemites proudly showed Lorraine vacant and crumbling buildings and closed or relo-cated businesses and bragged about what had once been there.

Even though the old Harlem was fading, a new Harlem was emerging and it was exciting, too. Lorraine felt a new energy replac-

A demonstration in Harlem during the 1920s

ing the old one of Harlem, powered by anger, disillusionment, and hopelessness. Most of what Lorraine knew about Harlem, she'd read in books and magazines, and of course, in the works of Langston Hughes, who was "the voice of Harlem." As a leading poet of the Harlem Renaissance, Hughes's voice had captured for three decades the dreams and realities of ordinary people who lived around 125th Street. Lorraine couldn't wait to experience firsthand all that Hughes had described — the good and the horrible. She was not disappointed.

She sucked in all the sounds, smells, and tastes the community had to offer, then exhaled them in a big gush of laughter, tears, and protest speeches. The streets of Harlem stimulated the activism that had been growing inside her since elementary school. In an unmailed letter to her former college roommate, Lorraine wrote:

> *I am considerably slimmer than you remember me, have stopped whacking my hair off and it's at some strange length, some of the blemishes have disappeared off my face and I think I smile less, but perhaps with more sincerity when I do . . . have learned to love clothes in a new way . . . life in a new way. I think I am a little different. Attend meetings almost every night, sing in a chorus, eat all the foreign foods in New York, usher at rallies, make street corner speeches in Harlem, sometimes make it up to the country on Sundays, go for long walks in Harlem and talk to my people about everything on the streets.*

One memorable event stood out as a poignant example of Lorraine's commitment to social reform. She attended the funeral of a black student protester who had been shot by a police officer during a demonstration. Appalled by the "official violence" that had taken the life of such a young man, Lorraine wrote: "You can't see his fists. They are under that part which is closed, but you get the feeling that they are balled up tight."

By then she was more convinced than ever that she wanted to be counted among those — "the younger, less docile generation" that "would respond with a cry for a militant student movement," against injustices whenever and wherever they existed.

Two people she'd met as a child re-entered her life during this period — Paul Robeson and W.E.B. DuBois. After taking a course in jewelry making and another in short story writing, Lorraine landed a job with *Freedom,* a left-wing, socialist, intellectual monthly that had recently been started by Paul Robeson. "I have finally stopped going to school and started working," she wrote to a friend. "I work for the new Negro paper, FREEDOM, which in its time in history ought to be *the* journal of Negro liberation . . . in fact it will be."

Lorraine had met Paul Robeson when she was a child in Chicago during the 1930s and '40s. She had seen him perform in *The Tempest* and *Othello,* at the peak of his career. Lorraine's father, however, had admired Robeson because of his involvement in the civil rights struggle and because he was one of the early advocates of African independence.

Born on April 9, 1898, in Princeton, New Jersey, Robeson entered Rutgers University in 1915 on an academic scholarship. He distinguished himself as both an athlete and scholar and graduated with Phi Beta Kappa honors in 1919. While playing professional sports, he earned his law degree from Columbia University in New York, but there were very few openings for black lawyers in corporate America.

Paul Robeson, the famed actor, activist, and publisher of *Freedom*

Robeson's wife, Eslanda (Essie) Goode, encouraged him to perform in a YWCA play which was so well-reviewed he landed parts in Broadway and London productions. In 1922 he was given the role of Jim Harris in Eugene O'Neill's *All God's Chullin Got Wings*, and later he played the part of Brutus Jones in O'Neill's *The Emperor Jones*. He made history in the 1940s when he became the first black actor to play the leading role opposite a white woman in Shakespeare's *Othello*.

As a performing artist, Robeson was brilliant; as an activist, he was bold. Through the years, he had become increasingly more outspoken about the failings of the United States, which he called a "democracy in default."

At the 1949 World Peace Conference in Paris, Robeson declared that it would be "unthinkable" for African Americans "to go to war on behalf of those who have oppressed [them] for generations . . ."

Such comments, said on the eve of the Korean War, made Robeson one of the most controversial black persons in America and a target of the McCarthy inquiries.

Some people considered a "red takeover" inevitable unless radical measures were taken to stop the infiltration of communists in the United States. The House Un-American Activities Committee (HUAC, pronunced *Hew-Ack*) was organized to investigate the communist threat. The committee called hundreds of people to testify before them, always asking, "Are you, or have you ever been, a member of the Communist Party?" Most of the people answered no, and they were telling the truth. But nobody believed them, reasoning that the committee wouldn't have called them if there hadn't been a good reason. That was precisely the problem; HUAC had the authority to question citizens' loyalty on the flimsiest of evidence. The abuses of power were astounding. Anybody who criticized the government for anything became suspect and was quickly labeled "a real and present danger to the security of the United States." Hundreds of people's lives were destroyed by the hysteria against communists that turned friends against neighbors. People were afraid to say anything that might make them appear "un-American."

But not Paul Robeson. His career gave him an international platform from which to present his ideas, and he did. In a regular column, "Here's My Story," he forthrightly detailed his personal battle against the "twin evils" of racism and discrimination.

In retaliation the State Department pulled his passport, forcing him to fight for his freedom to travel. Lorraine joined the staff of *Freedom* while Robeson was busy defending himself before HUAC.

Louis Burnham, the editor who hired Lorraine, recognized that in spite of her youth and inexperience, she would bring a fresh and energetic perspective to the magazine. Of Burnham, who became her mentor, Lorraine wrote: "The things he taught me were great things: that all racism was rotten, white or black; that everything is political; that people tend to be indescribably beautiful and uproariously funny."

Lorraine quickly embraced *Freedom*'s editorial policy, which was to keep the African-American community informed about issues ignored by the mainstream press, especially the exploitation of African countries by colonial powers, Senator Joseph McCarthy's intimidation of American citizens, and racism.

Freedom's office on 125th Street was a gathering place for some of the brightest minds of the day, many of whom regularly contributed articles to the paper. The writers included the artist Charles White; actress, humorist, and playwright Alice Childress; novelist John O. Killens; and W.E.B. DuBois. Getting reacquainted with DuBois while at *Freedom* was a real pleasure for Lorraine.

Born to a family of free blacks on February 23, 1868, in Great Barrington, Massachusetts, DuBois had earned his undergraduate degree from Fisk University and became the first black to earn a Ph.D. in History from Harvard. DuBois was thrust into national leadership after the publication of his book *The Souls of Black Folks* (1903), in which he launched his attack against the "accommodationist" philosophy of Booker T. Washington, whose speech known as "the Atlanta Compromise" had angered and disturbed many blacks. The races could be as separate as the fingers on the hand, in all things social, Washington

W.E.B. DuBois, author of *The Souls of Black Folks* and a co-founder of the NAACP

had said, but one as the fist during times of national need. Immediately, whites proclaimed Washington "the" leader of all African Americans, a notion that infuriated DuBois. Black people do not think with a collective brain, DuBois argued, so it is impossible for them to have one leader.

In 1909 DuBois and several other "radical" blacks joined forces with "progressive" northern whites to form the National Association for the Advancement of Colored People, the NAACP, to legally challenge the disfranchisement of African Americans. DuBois left his teaching post at Atlanta College to become the editor of *Crisis* magazine, the publishing arm of the NAACP. In a 1915 *Crisis* editorial, "The Immediate Programs of the American Negro," DuBois clearly stated what the struggle was about.

We need not waste time by seeking to deceive our enemies into thinking we are going to be content with half of a loaf . . . The American Negro demands equality — political equality, industrial equality and social equality; and he is never going to rest satisfied with anything less. He demands this in no spirit of braggadocio and with no obsequious envy, but with an absolute measure of self defense and the only one to assure the darker races their ultimate survival on earth.

DuBois never wavered from these goals, even though by the mid-1950s he was under attack for his outspoken criticism of the government's foreign and domestic policies regarding people of color around the world. He, too, had been called before HUAC to answer charges that he was a member of the Communist Party.

"I have faced during my life many unpleasant experiences: the growl of a mob, the personal threat of murder, the scowling distaste of an audience," DuBois wrote. "But nothing cowed me as that day, November 8, 1951, when I took my seat in a Washington courtroom as an indicted criminal." Both DuBois and Robeson (a co-defendant) had expressed privately that while they agreed in principle with many socialist ideas, they weren't members of the Communist Party. But they stubbornly refused to answer when asked, if in fact, they were party members. They took protection under the Fifth Amendment.

A sampling of Lorraine's *Freedom* articles reflects the influence of her two mentors, as well as her love of the arts, African history, politics, freedom for people of color on a national and international basis, and an emerging interest in women's rights.

In her articles about Africa, Lorraine was able to share her knowledge of and appreciation for the continent's past and its present growth and development. In a piece titled "Kenya's Kikuyu," Lorraine focused on contemporary Africa, describing the trial of her hero Jomo Kenyatta, who had been jailed for his participation in the Kikuyu revolt against British domination. She ingeniously used one of Kenyatta's fables from *Facing Mount Kenya*, to explain colonialism and its eventual fate. This is a summary of the story:

Once there was a man who made friends with an elephant. When the rains came, the man let the elephant put his head inside his hut to stay dry and warm. Soon the elephant pushed his whole body inside the man's house and the man was forced out into the storm. The man pleaded for justice, but the elephant now claimed the man's hut and refused to move. Still the man tried to negotiate a settlement, asking first for the elephant to leave the hut or at least share the hut so that they both might be dry. But the elephant insisted that the man had no claim to his own house, and the elephant even passed laws legalizing his rights to take the man's house and solicited the help of the snake, crocodile and baboon to help him enforce the unjust laws. Grown weary from the struggle, the man built a fire and burned the hut, with the elephant inside.

Lorraine wrote several other thoughtful articles about the contemporary Egyptian freedom movement, the quest for human rights in Sierra Leone, and about Ghana and its new prime minister, Kwame Nkrumah. Dr. Nkrumah, who had been a student of Uncle Leo's at Howard, took control of the recently freed nation in 1951 and began a vigorous program to advance Ghana's social and economic services.

As a representative from *Freedom*, Hansberry attended and reported on a women's conference, held in Washington, D.C., in the fall of 1951. Over 132 black women, calling themselves "Sojourners for Truth," rallied to unite their voices against war and racial discrimination. It is interesting that the women were not demanding rights for themselves, but equal opportunity and justice for their husbands, brothers, uncles, and sons. The women were angry that the men in

Kwame Nkrumah, the first Prime Minister of Ghana after independence

their lives were expected to fight in Korea when they were victims of brutal lynchings and other forms of discrimination at home. Although a number of political leaders attended, such as Mary McLeod Bethune, most of the participants were housewives and mothers who were fed up with racism.

After visiting Anacostia, the home of Frederick Douglass, the delegates took courage from the words of Sojourner Truth, a nineteenth-century abolitionist and one of the earliest American feminists, who said: "God will not hold with wrong no matter how right you think you be."

Meanwhile, Robeson had hoped to attend the 1952 Intercontinental Peace Congress in Montevideo, Uruguay, where 250 delegates from eight South American countries and the United States planned to protest the Korean War, but the State Department would not release Robeson's passport. Lorraine was sent in his place.

In spite of the bumpy flight that marked the beginning of her lifelong fear of flying, she represented Robeson at the conference. In a special session for women she was given a standing ovation and presented with a bouquet of flowers and a handcrafted doll. It was exciting to hear the audience chant, "Viva Robeson! Viva Robeson!"

Even though she was just twenty-two years old, Lorraine's poise and confidence earned her a promotion to associate editor when she returned. She was called an "intellectual revolutionary" for her articles on police harassment, discrimination in hotel management, and poor schools. Part of her new job description was to review the arts. In "Negroes Cast in Same Old Roles" Lorraine denounced *Amos 'n' Andy* as the "most despised anti-Negro show in the history of radio." She concluded that "the longer the concept of the half-idiot subhuman can be kept up, the easier to justify economic and every other kind of discrimination, so rampant in this country."

One of her most fiery reviews was of Richard Wright's book, *The Outsider* (1953). Wright (1908–1960) was considered by many to be the most eloquent spokesman for the African-American poor and underprivileged. He had established his reputation with his first novel, the powerful *Native Son,* which was followed quickly by the autobiographical *Black Boy.* Later, he published *The Outsider,* which was a philosophical piece.

Hansberry wrote:

> The Outsider *is a story of sheer violence, death and disgusting spectacle written by a man who has seemingly come to despise humanity . . . Wright has lost his own dignity and destroyed his talents. He exalts brutality and nothingness. He negates the reality of our struggle for freedom and yet worked energetically on behalf of our oppressors.*

This was a harsh analysis of a popular and much-admired writer. In 1967 Harold Cruse lambasted Hansberry's review of Wright's work in a widely acclaimed and influential book, *The Crisis of the Negro Intellectual:*

> *One could indeed criticize* The Outsider, *but what could this young woman from upper-class colored Chicago ever know about what led Richard Wright to write such a book? What could she possibly have known about the "misery, humiliation, violence and resentment of Wright's early life in the south," described in his autobiographical* Black Boy?

Richard Wright, the author of *Native Son* and *Black Boy*

Cruse's criticism raised an issue that was to dog Hansberry for some time. Since her own personal background had not been rooted in the realities of black poverty, Cruse and others asked how could she write knowledgeably about that experience? How could she dare to criticize the writings of those who had grown up, as Wright had, under the worst conditions of racial oppression and economic hardship when she had not lived it? Lorraine vehemently disagreed with these views. In her mind, all black people, regardless of their education and economic status, shared a common history and a common enemy: racism.

In her review of Wright's book, Lorraine did not focus on what caused him to write the book, but on the effect she thought the book would have on others and on the movement for civil rights. Her opinion of literature's purpose and responsibility was sharply different from that of many of her critics. Her associations and her work at *Freedom* had instilled in her a deep awareness of what she termed "literature's social accountability and ethical obligations."

Other *Freedom* articles help to reveal Hansberry's growth as a writer and maturity as a thinker. For example, she was by then an avowed atheist, yet she clearly understood the role of black churches in the civil rights movement — even before the emergence of Martin Luther King, Jr. In a comprehensive article titled "Church Always Led Freedom's Struggles" she explained:

> *Torn from their own civilization and land more than three centuries ago to face a new and strange world — in chains — African ancestors soon threw themselves eagerly into the Christian religion to which they were exposed in America. They adapted this religion to their needs, and discarding the chaff which they found in their white slave masters' actions, they embraced the wheat of brotherly love of Jesus and took courage and hope from his suffering and inspiring militancy.*
>
> *The Negro church became part and parcel of the Negro people's fight for freedom and has remained in a position of leadership insofar as it has continued to associate itself with the aspiration and continued struggles of its people — for freedom and a better life.*

In her free time, Lorraine completed a community project on an African-American journalist and anti-lynching crusader, Ida B. Wells. She wrote a collection of stories about other African-American heroes for children, and continued to speak to groups and participate in protests. In fact, it was during a 1951 demonstration against discriminatory practices on the New York University basketball team that she met her future husband, Robert Nemiroff.

13

Robert (Bob) Nemiroff was an aspiring writer and graduate student in English and history at New York University. Robert understood the devastating effects of McCarthyism. His parents, Mae and Motya

Nemiroff, were Russian Jewish immigrants who had prospered in the restaurant business. During the McCarthy era anybody Russian — even a reputable American citizen — might be suspected of being a communist sympathizer. The Nemiroffs' restaurants suffered some losses, because people were fearful of associating with or being seen in the company of a possible communist. Russians who spoke with even the slightest accent found themselves shunned by former neighbors, clients, and business contacts.

Lorraine and Bob enjoyed many of the same things, but most of all they shared a love of words and an unconditional commitment to peace and justice. Lorraine wrote home about Robert — Bob — which made Nannie Hansberry very happy.

"When Mother heard that Lorraine was moving evicted families' furniture back into their apartments to protest unfair rental rates, I thought she would have a fit," said Mamie. "Frankly, I was pretty proud of my little sister . . . and deep down, so was Mother. But, more than anything Mother wanted Lorraine to settle down and get married." Nannie was delighted when Lorraine's letters spoke about Robert more frequently.

Robert Nemiroff

Robert and Lorraine dated throughout the summer and fall, eating at ethnic restaurants, taking long walks together, and talking, talking endlessly about ideas. The day after Christmas 1952, she wrote to Bob, "I have finally admitted to myself that I do love you . . . and I am a writer. I am going to write . . ."

Shortly after her return to New York, they announced their engagement, which made Nannie happy although she was a bit concerned about the interracial marriage. In 1953 interracial marriages were uncommon, and in many states they were illegal. There might have been a problem if the two families had objected, but the Nemiroffs welcomed Lorraine into their family with love and admiration, and the Hansberrys accepted Robert unconditionally.

Mrs. Hansberry proudly invited a few family members and friends to the wedding of her daughter Lorraine Vivian at the family home at:

1145 Hyde Park Boulevard
Chicago, Illinois
on June 20, 1953
at 6:30 P.M.

The guests began arriving at six o'clock. The house was decorated with pink and white flowers; the guests included Robert's brother and sister and his best friend Burt D'Lugoff. They were escorted to their seats in the living room by Lorraine's brothers, Carl, Jr., and Perry. After the Nemiroffs and Nannie Hansberry had been escorted to their seats, the ceremony began. Robert and Reverend Archibald M. Carey (a minister who would later become U.S. delegate to the United Nations) stood in front of the white brick fireplace. Mamie, the matron of honor, entered first. It was hard to guess that less than twenty-four hours before the wedding the bride and groom had taken part in a nationwide demonstration.

The bride and groom had spent June 19th at the Chicago Federal Building, protesting the execution of Julius and Ethel Rosenberg,

A protest against the execution of Julius and Ethel Rosenberg

who had been convicted of selling atomic secrets to the Soviet Union. Similar demonstrations took place all over the country. A key theme during the rally speeches was that the Rosenbergs were victims of the Cold War "Red Scare" frenzy and the hysteria of McCarthyism. Despite efforts to save the Rosenbergs, the Supreme Court denied their appeal and President Dwight Eisenhower refused to grant them executive clemency. The executions took place at 8:04 and 8:11 P.M. Lorraine and Bob had thought about postponing their wedding, but neither of them wanted to disappoint their parents.

Lorraine marched into the room, looking radiant in Mamie's recycled white lace wedding dress, and became the wife of Robert Nemiroff. According to the *Chicago Defender,* "a lavish dinner party and reception followed."

A few weeks later, the newlyweds returned to New York and set up housekeeping in a second-floor apartment at 337 Bleeker Street in Greenwich Village which they shared with an "almost Collie," named

Spice (Spicy). Like a lot of Village walk-ups, the rooms were small, but "jammed with living." A visitor might find records and books on every tabletop, munchies on a plate, petty cash tossed in a bowl, and reproductions of Picasso, Gauguin, and Michelangelo on the wall.

A lot of changes took place during their first year of marriage. The Korean War ended on July 27, 1953, exactly three years after it had started. On May 17, 1954, the United States Supreme Court struck down the "separate but equal" doctrine of segregation, overruling the 1896 *Plessy v. Ferguson* decision. And, the United States Senate voted 67–22 to censure Senator Joseph McCarthy for abusing his power, although the anti-communist obsession persisted well into the 1980s.

Lorraine stopped working full-time for *Freedom,* but continued to contribute articles until it went bankrupt in 1955. Meanwhile, during 1953, Robert finished his Master's degree and worked as an editor and later the promotion director at Avon Books. Lorraine took a course in African history from Dr. DuBois, who, although acquitted of conspiring to overthrow the U.S. government, was still denied a passport. While the court battles continued, DuBois did what he loved best — teach black history.

Perhaps Lorraine enrolled in his course at the Jefferson School of Social Science to lend her support to a friend, or to prepare herself for several writing projects she had in mind. More than likely Lorraine saw it as an opportunity. Studying with DuBois would give her a rare and wonderful perspective on history, especially from a man who had helped shape it for nearly sixty-five years.

In order to have more writing time, Lorraine took part-time jobs with a furrier and a music production company. Both she and Robert longed for more time to work on the numerous projects they both had in process. According to biographer Anne Cheney, Bob was the "perfect husband" for Lorraine. He was himself a competent writer with a critical eye. Theirs was a partnership that was beneficial to them both. Lorraine trusted Bob and he respected her abilities, and they were both confident in their own abilities and secure in that relationship.

Their big break came as the result of a pop song, written by Bob and his best friend, Burt D'Lugoff. "Cindy, Oh Cindy" was released in August of 1956, and earned them $100,000. Without financial worries, Lorraine had no reason not to write. At first she was working on several plays, a novel, and an opera all at once, then she decided to focus her energies on a play which she had tentatively titled *The Crystal Stair,* a concept derived from a line in Langston Hughes's poem "Mother to Son."

Why Hansberry chose that particular line is unknown, but that she chose to use something from Hughes holds no mystery. Langston Hughes was one of Lorraine's literary heroes and with good reason. Since "The Negro Speaks of Rivers," Hughes's first poem, which was originally published in 1921 in *Crisis* magazine, he had become one of the most prolific and popular poets in America.

As long as Lorraine could remember, Hughes had been the premier black writer in the country and a personal favorite of hers and her father. She had discovered his work on her father's bookshelves when she was a child. She had even met the distinguished poet when he visited her home in Chicago.

Hughes was born in 1902 in Joplin, Missouri, the only son of Carrie and Nathaniel Hughes. He read to endure the overwhelming loneliness he experienced growing up in several mostly white, midwestern communities where there weren't many blacks living nearby. Often Langston was the only black child in his class — sometimes in the whole school. He made friends in books, where "if people suffered they [did so] in beautiful language, not in monosyllables, as [he] did in Kansas."

It was Langston's grandmother, an Oberlin College graduate, who introduced him to the Bible, which helped him develop a vivid imagination and an appreciation for beautiful language. She also introduced him to *Crisis* magazine and helped him learn about his his-

The poet Langston Hughes

tory. His grandmother also told him stories about proud black people who worked, schemed, or fought, but never cried.

As a writer, Langston Hughes championed the cause of hard-working fighters who never cried. He made heroes out of ordinary people whose courage and humor helped them triumph over adversity. Lorraine admired the way he captured the very essence of being black with flawless simplicity. It was this ability to write with an easy eloquence that separated Hughes from his contemporaries and earned him the respect and admiration of young writers like Lorraine.

14

Although Lorraine's writing was going well, there were times when her dialogue seemed contrived or the characters phony and she wanted to throw the whole manuscript in the trash. In fact in a fit of frustration she threw her play in the fireplace. But Robert retrieved it and put it away for a few days. Once she'd had a chance to think over the problems, Robert returned the manuscript to her and the work continued, the rapid tapping of her typewriter sounding steadily sometimes until two o'clock in the morning.

Other times when she needed to take a break, Lorraine took long walks in the Village, going nowhere in particular. Taking a walk in the Village could lead you in a hundred different directions — all of them interesting — especially to a writer.

In the early '50s the place to be was Greenwich Village. A Village address meant you were part of the trend-setting "beat generation" — a "beatnik." The Village population was comprised of creative people — musicians, writers, artists, and performers — who jammed hard in smoky nightclubs. Dancing — jumping around, getting hot and sweaty — was out, listening to the beat was in. The Village sound was jazz and the thing to be there was cool. Smoking was sophisticated and dressing down was *en vogue*. In Village language serious conversations were "heavy" and to understand was to "dig it."

During one of her strolls through the Village, Lorraine wandered into a studio theater where James Baldwin's play *Giovanni* was being performed. Baldwin's novel *Go Tell It on the Mountain* (1953) had received rave reviews and, indeed, he was destined to become one of the most powerful writers of the twentieth century, but some of his best works were yet to come.

A few big Hollywood and Broadway names had come to see Baldwin's play, and they hated it because it was about homosexuality, a taboo subject in the 1950s. But Hansberry, who had taken a seat in the back of the theater, stepped forward and said she liked the play very

James Baldwin made his reputation with the critically acclaimed novel *Go Tell It on the Mountain.*

much. At that time, Lorraine Hansberry wasn't a well-known writer either, but she was so articulate and persuasive she impressed everyone who was there.

Baldwin was grateful to her. "She seemed to speak to me," he said, ". . . with a gentleness and generosity never to be forgotten." Although they knew about each other, that was the first time Hansberry and Baldwin had ever met.

Within a few weeks, Lorraine finished her play. She stacked the pages neatly, then went into the living room and stretched out on the floor face down and savored the joy of completion. She wasn't researching it, writing it, or rewriting it anymore. She was finished! Little did she know, she was really just beginning.

After a dinner party at her home one evening in late 1957, Lorraine offered to read a scene or two from the play to the guests. She explained that she'd changed the title from *The Crystal Stair* to *A*

Raisin in the Sun, which was a line from another Hughes poem:

> *What happens to a dream deferred?*
> *Does it dry up*
> *Like a raisin in the sun?*
> *Or fester like a sore-*
> *And then run?*
> *Does it stink like rotten meat?*
> *Or crust and sugar over-*
>
> *Like a syrupy sweet?*
> *Maybe it just sags*
> *Like a heavy load.*
>
> *Or does it explode?*

Lorraine introduced her characters: the Youngers.

Lena (Mama) was the oldest member of the family; her son, Walter Lee, a thirty-five year old chauffeur was married to Ruth, a domestic worker. Lena's daughter, Beneatha, is a college student. Beneatha's two suitors are a Nigerian and a wealthy snob. Travis, Walter Lee and Ruth's ten-year old son, a white representative of the neighborhood association, and Bobo, a friend of Walter Lee's, helped round out the main characters.

TIME:	*1957*
PLACE:	*South Side of Chicago, U.S.A. . .*
SETTING:	*A small apartment where the Youngers live*

As the play opens, the members of a three-generational, working-class family, are in conflict about many things, but the most immediate tension centers around the $10,000 insurance money left to Lena Younger by her late husband, Big Walter.

Walter Lee, Lena's son, is full of anger and resentment, because at age thirty-five, he and his family are still living with his mother. He is stuck in a low-paying, unfulfilling job, and his wife and mother work as domestics to supplement his salary. And to complicate matters, his wife, Ruth, is pregnant. "Where will it sleep, on the roof?" Beneatha asks, ex-

pressing the frustration they all feel, because their small apartment is already overcrowded.

Beneatha, a young college student with a quick mind and a tongue to match, wants to go to medical school. She is exploring all kinds of new and interesting ideas that are often in conflict with her mother's traditional beliefs. Beneatha is also dating two men. Asagai, who is a handsome and sophisticated Nigerian, introduces Beneatha to African history and culture. He inspires her to become involved in the present-day struggle for African independence. George Murchison, on the other hand, is the perfect example of a chauvinistic bore. He pokes fun at Beneatha's "afro" hair style and arrogantly dismisses her interest in Africa as little more than a fad.

Walter wants to use the insurance money to invest in a liquor store. Beneatha, who is young and idealistic, has begun to question the existence of God and when Ruth considers an abortion and Walter Lee doesn't object, Lena is sure her family is falling apart. She puts a down payment on a house large enough for the family to be comfortable — "nothing fancy," but adequate. The house, however, is in an all-white neighborhood.

Instead of being happy, Walter Lee falls deeper and deeper into despair. After a confrontation between mother and son, Mama turns the family finances over to Walter Lee, with the understanding that he is to put enough away for Beneatha's medical school expenses, then with the rest he can do whatever he thinks is best for the family.

Walter Lee invests in a liquor store with two friends, Willie and Bobo, using all the cash, including Beneatha's medical school money. His spirits rise, and his failed marriage seems to be mending. The family is visited by Karl Lindner, a representative from the neighborhood association, who comes to the Younger's apartment, offering to buy their house back for more than what they'd paid, just to keep a black family from moving into the neighborhood. Walter Lee orders Lindner out of the house.

On moving day, Bobo comes to the apartment with the sad story that Willie has stolen all their money and disappeared. Walter Lee, ashamed and hurt, decides to take the association's offer. But when Lindner comes, Walter Lee is unable to accept the deal. Speaking as the head of his fam-

ily, Walter tells Lindner that he and his family aren't "looking for trou-
ble"; they aren't interested "in causes"; they just want to move into their
home and live in peace.

The play closes with the Youngers leaving the old apartment.

Lorraine hadn't intended to read the whole play, but her guests urged her to go on until she finished. Among the guests who were there that night was Philip Rose, a former concert baritone. Robert had run a music publishing company owned by Rose.

"I didn't get home until 4:30 A.M.," Rose said later. "Then I called Lorraine at nine the next morning, woke her up, and asked for an option to produce the play. She thought I had lost my mind."

But Rose was quite sane. Right away he contacted his actor-friend, Sidney Poitier, who after reading the work, agreed to play the part of Walter Lee Younger. Poitier suggested that Rose get Lloyd Richards, one of the few black directors in the business, to direct it.

Poitier was a hot item in 1958–59. Handsome, witty, and talented, he had given stunning performances on the stage and in films, including *Cry the Beloved Country,* a story set in South Africa. He had star status, even though he hadn't won the Academy Award for best actor yet.

Canadian-born Lloyd Richards had just been seen in the Broadway production of *The Egghead,* but he had always wanted to direct. There weren't too many opportunities on Broadway in the 1950s for a black director, so Richards jumped at this chance, even though the play was written by an untested playwright.

Everybody involved knew, especially the playwright, that *A Raisin in the Sun* wasn't going to be produced easily. Having strong actors express a desire to take part wasn't enough to get adequate financing. Rose couldn't find one big investor, but with the help of actor-activist, Harry Belafonte, Rose raised the seed money from small contributions made by one hundred and fifty investors. He was able to get the rest from a long-time friend, David Cogan, a tax accountant and fellow musician.

The remaining cast was selected and rehearsals began.

The part of Lena Younger (Mama) went to Claudia McNeil, who had twenty-three years of show business experience. She'd begun as a singer, but turned to acting, first appearing in Arthur Miller's *The Crucible.*

Ruby Dee was delighted when she was given the part of Ruth Younger, the long-suffering wife of Walter Lee. She'd performed opposite Poitier the year before in the film, *The Edge of Night.* She and

A rehearsal of the original cast of *A Raisin in the Sun*

Ruby Dee with new cast members Frances Williams and Ossie Davis

her husband Ossie Davis were already good friends of Hansberry and Nemiroff, having participated in protests together many times.

Diana Sands, a native New Yorker, had begun acting at age fourteen. At sixteen, she appeared in an out-of-town production of *The Madwoman of Chaillot.* Getting the part of Beneatha was a real break for her.

Lou Gossett, Jr., who later won an Academy Award for his role in *An Officer and a Gentleman,* was a rising star in 1958. A graduate of New York University with a B.A. degree in dramatic arts, Gossett had made his career debut in the lead role of an off-Broadway production. He was selected to play Beneatha's boyfriend, George Murchison.

Ivan Dixon's small part in *Something of Value* helped secure him the role of Beneatha's other romantic interest, Joseph Asagai, a Nigerian student. Fourteen-year-old Glynn Thurman bagged the part of ten-year-old Travis Younger, and John Fiedler, the only white person in the play, was given the part of Karl Lindner. Lonne Elder III, Ed Hall, and Douglass Turner rounded out the cast as Bobo and the moving men.

"Lorraine allowed herself to be excited when they actually started rehearsing," remembered Mamie. "The whole family was excited. This was our little sister's play, starring Sidney Poitier! What could be better than that?"

During the weeks of rehearsal, Lorraine made revisions, did some trimming, and smoothed out the rough spots in several scenes. Meanwhile Rose had to clear the next hurdle, which was finding a theater that would accept the play. *A Raisin in the Sun* was about a black family, with an all-black leading cast, written by a black playwright, directed by a black man. There wasn't a theater in New York that would touch it. All those connected with the project had confidence in its merit, so Rose decided to hold tryout performances in New Haven, Philadelphia, and Chicago. If the reviews were good there, then Broadway would have no choice but to yield to popular opinion.

The play opened on a frosty New Haven night in January 1959 to hot reviews the next morning. It was also well-received in Philadelphia in February. James Baldwin, who saw the play in Philadelphia, was overjoyed that so many black people had a reason to come to the theater. While some people believed they came only to see Poitier, Baldwin disagreed. "They were there," he said, "because the life on that stage said something to them concerning their own lives."

At a reception following the opening, Hansberry and Baldwin got reacquainted. The two of them picked up where they had left off at his production in the Village. They were rapidly becoming good friends. It always surprised Baldwin — but not Lorraine — that even though they grew up in completely different circumstances, they had a great deal in common.

Baldwin was born in 1924 in Harlem to an unwed mother. His stepfather, David Baldwin, was a storefront preacher whose mental health was unstable, which affected his general health. He died when James was in his early teens. Although Baldwin felt responsible for caring for his mother and eight brothers and sisters, he also wanted to be a writer. His determination impressed Richard Wright, who became his mentor and encouraged him. By the late 1950s, Baldwin's novels and essays had earned him the honor of being one of America's most talented writers. Just as her opinion had meant a lot to Baldwin on that evening in the Village, his praise of her play was music to her ears.

In the playwright's hometown, Hansberry stood to take her bows, uncharacteristically dressed in a stunning black dress. Mamie admitted during an interview years later that she had bought the dress for the Chicago premiere.

> *I asked Lorraine what she was going to wear. She looked at me with that 'I-don't-know-look.' Perhaps worrying about what to wear to an affair seems trivial today, but I felt it was important at that time. She told me to "take care of it for me," and of course I did — gladly.*

And yes, Mamie arranged for Lorraine to get her hair styled and applied her makeup. "Lorraine would have just as soon worn blue jeans."

Langston Hughes attended the Chicago opening and sent Lorraine a note of praise. Lorraine was proudest of her mother's approval. Lorraine had written Nannie tentatively on opening night in New Haven:

Dear Mother,

The actors are very good and the director is a very talented man — so if it is a poor show, I won't be able to blame a soul, but your youngest daughter.

Mama, it is a play that tells the truth about people — Negroes and life and I think it will help a lot of people understand how we are just as complicated as they are — and just as mixed up — but above all, that we have among our miserable and downtrodden ranks — people who are the very essence of human dignity. That is what, after all the laughter and tears, the play is supposed to say. I hope it will make you very proud. . . .

"Mother was stunned by Lorraine's talent," said Mamie. "After the play she just kept nodding her head in that way that meant she was pleased." Anybody with eyes could have seen how much it meant to Lorraine and her mother to share that special moment.

Since *A Raisin in the Sun* was getting rave reviews on the road, the Shuberts invited the play to open at their theater on Broadway. The arrangements were made and the play opened on March 11, 1959, at the Ethel Barrymore Theater on Broadway — a milestone.

15

The night *A Raisin in the Sun* premiered on Broadway, the history books were rewritten and a lot of stereotypes about blacks were dimmed if not altogether erased. The moment Lloyd Richards came out on stage following the performance, the audience stood and roared their approval. After the crowd had applauded for a full fifteen minutes, Sidney Poitier went into the audience and escorted the playwright to the stage. Nannie Hansberry was heard by a *Vogue* magazine reporter to say, "That's my daughter." While the theater shook with another round of thunderous applause, Lorraine Hansberry took her bows as the first black woman to have a play produced on Broadway.

In the audience that night also was Alice Childress, the first black woman to have a play produced off-Broadway, *Trouble in Mind,* which had won an Obie in 1955. Not present, but standing with her in spirit, were other black women dramatists who had blazed the trail for Hansberry. Angelina Grimke's *Rachel* was the first black play on record performed by blacks in the twentieth century, March 3, 1916, in

A poster for the Broadway hit

Washington, D.C., Alice Dunbar Nelson (former wife of the deceased poet, Paul Laurence Dunbar) wrote *Mine Eyes Have Seen the Glory* in 1918 to protest the treatment of black soldiers who were fighting in Europe for freedom, yet whose families didn't have freedom at home. Mary Burrill in *They That Sit in Darkness* advanced the cause of birth control, especially for poor women. Between 1920–50, Marita Bonner wrote *The Purple Flower,* Zora Neale Hurston and Langston Hughes collaborated on *Mule Bone,* and Georgia Douglas Johnson's *A Saturday Morning in the South* confronted lynching and racial violence head-on.

All these playwrights had offered alternatives to the degrading minstrel show stereotypes, but none of them had reached Broadway. Lorraine made it, and in so doing had scored a victory for them all. Her recognition validated the work of other women who had been denied access to Broadway because of racism and sexism.

On April 7, 1959, six weeks shy of her twenty-ninth birthday, Lorraine Hansberry won the prestigious New York Drama Critics Circle Award as the best play of the year, edging out plays such as Tennessee Williams's *Sweet Bird of Youth,* Archibald MacLeish's *JB,* and Eugene O'Neill's *A Touch of the Poet.* She was the youngest American playwright, the fifth woman, and the first black dramatist to win the coveted award.

In her acceptance speech she said, "I cannot adequately tell you what recognition and tribute mean to the young writer and, I am sure, to the young artist of all fields. One works, one dreams, and, if one is lucky, one actually produces. But true fulfillment only comes when our fellows say: 'Ah, we understand, we appreciate, we enjoy . . .' "

The cards, letters, and telegrams written by Hansberry admirers poured in by the hundreds. Her private life was invaded by requests for public interviews and appearances, but at first she didn't seem to mind. She enthusiastically told an interviewer that her success felt "wonderful, it's wonderful . . . I'm enjoying every bit of it. I've tried to go to everything I've been invited to and — I shouldn't even say this on the air — but so far I've tried to answer every piece of correspondence I get . . ."

Over the next few years, Lorraine answered letters from fans all over the globe, from Hollywood celebrities, housewives, students, fellow writers, and teachers. In a letter to a Mr. Chuchevalec who had translated *A Raisin in the Sun* into Czech, Lorraine stated: "My only sadness is that my cultural illiteracy will not allow me to read it in what, I am told, is your excellent translation."

In a letter written to Mme. Chen Jui-Lan, a professor at Peking University in China, Lorraine expressed her concerns about the lack of exchange between African American and Asian, specifically Chinese, playwrights.

We are, in the professional theater here [in the United States], obsessed with the least murmur in the European theater, but the art of Asia (excepting Japanese architecture, flower arrangement and kimono and an

Lorraine Hansberry, successful playwright

occasional touring Balinese dance troupe) remains out of the ken of even
those who consider themselves sophisticated in terms of world culture. The
present political chasm between our two nations has not diminished that
deplorable state of affairs. But, by all means, let you and I extend corre-
spondence to penetrate all that ignorance.

Hansberry and Mme. Chen Jui-Lan corresponded regularly until
Hansberry's death.

16

A Raisin in the Sun was different from any other play that had ever been
produced on Broadway, so naturally it was closely scrutinized by the media. And, of course, everything the playwright said was also analyzed.
Interviews with television reporter Mike Wallace and radio talk-show
host Studs Terkel, in addition to reviews, speeches, and scores of newspaper and magazine articles serve as the primary sources of Hansberry's public statements.

   Not all the reviews and criticisms of *Raisin* were good, which
Hansberry fully expected. What she didn't expect were the gross misconceptions that developed about herself and her work. For example,
she seemed deeply concerned that some whites just "didn't get it."
The white, male-dominated press applauded *Raisin* for not being a
"Negro play" but one that was *universal,* which implied that her black
characters could be replaced with white characters and the story
would be the same. She agreed in part, saying, "I don't think there is
anything more universal in the world than man's oppression to
man . . ." but Hansberry refused to allow others to define the "universal" meaning of her play. She insisted that "one of the most sound
ideas in dramatic writing is that, in order to create the universal, you
must pay very great attention to the specific." Hansberry argued that

her play was most definitely about a very specific black family who lived on the South Side of Chicago. In that sense it was a very "Negro play."

Repeatedly, Hansberry tried to clarify her intentions: "The thing I tried to show," she said, "was the many gradations even in one Negro family, the clash of the old and new, but most of all the unbelievable courage of the Negro people." Still the misconceptions persisted. Whites embraced the play without fully understanding its implications, but she was equally distressed that many blacks attacked the play simply because whites liked it.

Some black critics thought the playwright had "sought integration through the whitening of her characters." This initial misunderstanding led many people to believe that Hansberry's goal was to "convince whites that blacks were exactly like them, and that therefore full integration could take place without seriously disturbing the status quo or forcing hard sacrifices."

Margaret Just Butcher in "Postscript 1971" in *The Negro in American Culture* said although *Raisin* involved black people, it dealt "with common problems confronting a family that happened to be black." Other more militant voices accused the playwright of being too bourgeois and questioned how a middle-class intellectual could be sensitive to the needs of poor blacks. To which the artist responded:

> *I come from an extremely comfortable background, materially speaking. And yet, we live in a ghetto . . . which automatically means intimacy with all classes and all kinds of experiences. It's not any more difficult for me to know the people I wrote about than it is for me to know members of my family. This is one of the things that the American experience has meant to Negroes. We are* one *people.*

Hansberry made no apologies for her work then and it doesn't need any today. *A Raisin in the Sun* is a classic that has survived the test of time. Even some of her former critics have changed their position.

Another critic of *Raisin* was poet and playwright Amiri Baraka (then Leroi Jones). By 1979 he, too, had changed his mind, saying he and other young militants missed the essence of the work. He explained:

> *What is most telling about our ignorance is that Hansberry's play still remains overwhelmingly popular and evocative of black and white reality, and the masses of black people dug it true . . . the concerns I once dismissed as "middle class — buying a house and moving into 'white folks' neighborhoods" — are actually reflective of the essence of black people's striving and the will to defeat segregation, discrimination, and national oppression. There is no such thing as a "white folks' neighborhood" except to racists and to those submitting to racism.*

Perhaps Ed Siegel's review in the *Boston Globe* of the 1989 "American Playhouse" production of the play summarizes the lasting importance of Hansberry's contribution to drama and the continued misunderstanding that concerned Hansberry after the original production. "*A Raisin in the Sun* is not the tame, middle-class play captured by the Sidney Poitier movie," Siegel wrote. Hansberry never intended the Youngers to be a middle-class family. Siegel added that the play was "a major American work of art, as gritty as it is poetic, as specific as it is universal, and as contemporary as it is — and the word is not used loosely — visionary." On this point there is no disagreement.

17

Part of Hansberry's greatness lies in the way she involves her audience in a good story. She makes them care about what happens to her characters. Then she skillfully presents her ideas *through* them. The best way to grasp the playwright's social and political concerns is to study her characters.

As so many authors do, Hansberry used members of her family as skeletal models for the characters in *Raisin*. The similarities between Nannie and Mama Younger and Carl Hansberry and Big Walter are obvious. Walter Lee, Jr., and Lena are composites of Hansberry's brothers, their wives, and Mamie, while Beneatha is the playwright herself. Asagai and Murchison, Beneatha's rival boyfriends, are derived from young men Hansberry had met in Chicago, in college, or in New York. Here the similarities end.

Hansberry always believed there was a "flaw" in her play because there was no primary character from which all the action radiated. She believed good plays had one point-of-view character who was the center around which all the action evolved. "A central character as such is certainly lacking from *Raisin*," she wrote. In her opinion, neither Walter Lee nor Mama is strong enough to dominate the play. Lena Younger (Mama) is one of the most interesting of Hansberry's characters to analyze. Maybe it is because she was and continues to be controversial.

Lena and Big Walter represent the generation of Southern immigrants who came to Chicago, seeking a better life for themselves and their children. Lorraine saw hundreds of women like Mama, standing at the bus stop, shopping at the market. Mama has the characteristic "mother wit" — a natural ability attributed to people who have learned how to survive without a formal education. City living has not been "a crystal stair" for Lena Younger, but it has not left her bitter or angry.

Big Walter is not an onstage character, but he has an important role in the story. Based on what his family says about him, we know that Big Walter had been "unfaithful" to Lena, "hard-headed" and sometimes "mean," but in spite of having these "faults," he also had been a caring father. "Seem like God didn't see fit to give the black man nothing, but dreams," Lena repeated the words he'd spoken to her, " — but He did give us children to make them dreams seem worth while."

Some people argue that Lena is a prototype (and stereotype)

A scene from *A Raisin in the Sun,* with Ossie Davis as Walter Lee Younger

of the African-American "matriarch," a mother who dominates her daughter, intimidates her daughter-in-law, spoils her grandson, and emasculates her son. But Hansberry refuted that definition of her character. "On balance," she said, "the development of strong black women was a gain for the entire race, affirming that the would-be castigators of black men were not black women but the practitioners and enforcers of white racism."

In her 1959 Studs Terkel interview and in a speech on "The Origin of Character," Hansberry further defended the black matriarch, saying that women like Lena Younger were the backbone of the race, a role thrust on them since slavery. Black mothers, in her opinion, were

> *the bulwark of the Negro family since slavery; the embodiment of the Negro will to transcendence. It is she who, in the mind of the Black poet, scrubs the floors of a nation in order to create Black diplomats and university professors. It is she who, while seeming to cling to traditional restraints, drives the young on into the fire hoses and one day simply refuses to move to the back of the bus in Montgomery.*

Author-editor Lerone Bennett made an interesting observation that also dispels the matriarchal stereotype. "Father Younger [Big Walter] was a very strong man," says Bennett, "and the play clearly indicates that it was impossible for Mama Younger to dominate [him]."

As the play begins, Big Walter has died, leaving his wife a $10,000 insurance policy, which guarantees that his family will have some of the things he had been unable to give them while he was alive. In 1959, $10,000 was a large amount of money, considering the average house in Chicago sold for $7,500; a new Chevy Impala cost about $1,600, and a public school teacher's salary was about $3,000 a year.

Harold Cruse, Hansberry's most persistent critic, and others used the insurance policy to prove that the Youngers did not represent the working class. "How could a poor ghetto family of Southern origins come by a $10,000 insurance policy?" Cruse asked. Obviously, they didn't know the phenomenon of the "penny policy."

In 1898–99, several black investors established the North Carolina Mutual Insurance Company of Durham for the purpose of providing low-cost life insurance to African Americans. The policies — which by the 1950s ranged from $500–$2,000 — were an instant success among the poor. For literally a few pennies a week a father was guaranteed enough benefits to have a decent burial and to leave a small "inheritance" behind for his family's future. So, it was not unusual for poor blacks with low-paying jobs to have large amounts of insurance coverage, because it provided the security in death they were often unable to provide for their families in life.

Granted, it was an extraordinary feat for Big Walter to keep the premiums paid on a $10,000 policy, but certainly it was not extraordinary that he had a policy of that size. Lena gives us more information about her husband when she says after the death of their third child, Big Walter had worked "hisself to death . . . fighting his own war with this here world that took his baby from him." One literary critic suggests that Walter Younger's death was an "unconsciously calculated form of protracted suicide."

If the assumption is correct and Big Walter was the head of the household, then the act of leaving Lena the beneficiary of the policy makes her the head of the family. Big Walter could have just as easily divided the money, leaving his adult son and wife equal portions. Since Lena holds the purse strings, it is hard for her son to cut the apron strings, and that is the source of the conflict.

There are several scenes that show Lena stoically playing the hand life has dealt her the best way she knows how — making the family the center of her life and keeping her needs simple and her beliefs firmly rooted in practicality and faith. She is content that her children don't have to worry about being lynched or beaten, which in itself was a victory. "We have a roof over our heads and something to eat," she says, trying to understand why this isn't enough for her children.

In the classic scene from Act I, Hansberry immediately establishes the conflict between the older generation represented by Lena and Beneatha, a thoroughly "modern" woman. Beneatha says she wants to be a doctor. Mama Lena responds, "God willing, you'll be a doctor . . ." indicating that while she accepts the revolutionary idea that a woman — a poor black woman — can be a doctor, the outcome will be determined by a higher authority.

BENEATHA

Mama, you don't understand. It's all a matter of ideas, and God is just one idea I don't accept. It's not important. I am not going out and be immoral or commit crimes because I don't believe in God. I don't even think about it. It's just that I get tired of Him getting credit for all the things the human race achieves through its own stubborn effort. There simply is no blasted God — there is only man and it is he who makes miracles.

> (*Mama absorbs this speech, studies her daughter and rises slowly and crosses to Beneatha and slaps her powerfully across the face. After, there is only silence and the daughter drops her eyes from her mother's face and Mama is very tall before her.*)

MAMA

Now say after me, in my mother's house there is still God.

> (*There is a long pause and Beneatha stares at the floor wordlessly. Mama repeats the phrase with precision and cool emotion.*)

In my mother's house there is still God.

BENEATHA

In my mother's house there is still God.

> (*A long pause*)

MAMA

> (*Walking away from Beneatha, too disturbed for triumphant posture. Stopping and turning back to her daughter.*)

There are some ideas we ain't going to have in this house. Not long as I am at the head of this family.

BENEATHA

Yes, ma'am.

It is interesting to note then, and even today, during the face-slapping scene, many black and white women who were teenagers in the 1950s nod their heads in understanding of Mama Younger's response. They don't necessarily see it as a negative exchange, as many younger women do, and neither did Hansberry, who uses the daughter-in-law to put a cap on the confrontation: "What you did was childish," Ruth told Beneatha, "and you got treated like a child."

In the highly charged second scene in Act I, the generation gap widens and the tension mounts when Walter Lee expresses his hopes to use his father's insurance money to buy a partnership in a liquor store. Lena misses the intense need that Walter Lee has to be an independent person, successful enough to provide for his family. Convinced that selling liquor would be an immoral venture, Lena rejects the idea, saying, "Well, whether they drinks it or not ain't none of my business. But whether I go into business selling it to 'em *is,* and I don't want that on my ledger this late in life."

Sidney Poitier playing
Walter Lee Younger

Lena is trying to hold the family together, but the harder she tries, the more they seem to pull away. When Lena learns that her daughter-in-law is pregnant and planning to have an abortion, the rebellion of her children seems complete. "No . . . something has changed," she says.

> *In my time we was worried about not being lynched and getting to the North if we could and how to stay alive and still have a pinch of dignity too . . . Now here come you and Beneatha — talking 'bout things we ain't never even thought about hardly, me and your daddy. You ain't satisfied or proud of nothing we done. I mean that you had a home; and that we kept you out of trouble till you was grown; that you didn't have to ride to work on the back of nobody's streetcar — You my children — but how different we done become.*

To which Walter Lee answers, "You just don't understand, Mama, you just don't understand."

When Mama sees that her own demands are destroying her family, especially her son, she reveals her true strength of character, and gives him the rest of the money and passes the mantle to her son. He is now the head of the family, "like you supposed to be."

When Walter loses the money that has been entrusted to him, and all the family's dreams seem to be shattered, Beneatha rails against her brother, but in one of the most touching scenes in the play, Lena admonishes her daughter not to judge her brother until she had measured him right.

> *Child, when do you think is the time to love somebody the most? When they done good and made things easy for everybody? Well, then, you ain't through learning — because that ain't the time at all. It's when he's at his lowest and can't believe in hisself 'cause the world done whipped him so! When you start measuring somebody, measure him right, child, measure him right.*

Convinced at first that he should take the buy-back money from Karl Lindner, the white property owners' representative, Walter Lee changes his mind at the last moment and declares that he and his family will move into the house they have bought. Lindner tries to side-step Walter Lee's decision to buy the house by appealing to Lena, who he believes is the real head of the family — one who will undercut her son's decision. But Lena dismisses Lindner with a wave of her hand:

> *My son said we was going to move and there ain't nothing left for me to say . . . You know how these young folks is nowadays, mister. Can't do nothing with 'em.*

The key word to understanding Mama Younger is *change*. It takes courage to change. Lena is able to accept her changing role in the family. But she also realizes that the family is going to have to be strong and unified if they are to survive in their new environment.

A lot of people thought that the play had a fairy tale ending, but actually it doesn't. Based on personal experiences, Hansberry knew that the Youngers were probably going to be met with open hostility in their new home. What Hansberry did was send the audience away feeling whatever this family would encounter, they could survive. In one of the several drafts of the play, Hansberry supports this idea in an exchange between Mama Lena and Walter Lee following Lindner's final visit.

MAMA
(*Not looking at him*):
I'm proud you my boy. (*Walter is silent*) 'Cause you got get up . . . and you got to try again. You understand. You got to have more sense with it — and I got to be more with you — but you got to try again. You understand?

WALTER
Yes, Mama. We going to be all right, Mama. You and me, I mean.

MAMA
(*Grinning at him*)
Yeah — if the crackers don't kill us all.

Lena's concerns are grounded in the reality of their situation. In a very early version, Hansberry ended the play with the family sitting in the darkness while their house is being attacked by an angry mob, recapturing, perhaps, from her memory the time when her family waited in the dark while an angry mob threatened them. But Hansberry changed it because the focus was wrong.

She developed her characters so well, we don't need to see the Youngers under attack to know that they are going to be just fine. In the final manuscript, the play ends with Lena leaving the apartment, then returning to get a small flower that has been growing in her window, which symbolizes strength, determination, growth, and change.

CHAPTER III

. . . AND DETERMINED

[African Americans] must concern themselves with every single means of struggle: legal, illegal, passive, active, violent and nonviolent . . . they must harass, debate, petition, give money to court struggles, sit-in, lie down, strike boycott, sing hymns, pray on steps — and shoot from their windows when the white racists come cruising through their communities.

LORRAINE HANSBERRY

18

1960.

Things were changing rapidly for Lorraine. Nobody had noticed when she'd come to New York in 1950. But a decade later she made headlines when she signed a contract to write the screenplay for the movie version of *A Raisin in the Sun.*

1960.

The lyrics of a popular song described the mood of the country: "The times, they are a-changing." Young people were "Dancing in the Streets" with Martha and the Vandellas, a hot new pop group on the Motown label, and men's hair was getting longer and women's skirts were getting shorter.

1960.

The nation was changing its attitudes about racism and discrimination. In 1960 the nation elected a new president, John F. Kennedy, the first Catholic to be elected to the office. *Who next?* people wondered. If Americans were willing to elect a Catholic, then perhaps they would consider a Jew, a woman, a black?

Jim Crowism had been under attack all during the 1950s. The 1954 *Brown v. Board of Education of Topeka* Supreme Court decision that struck down the "separate but equal" doctrine had been a strong indicator that institutionalized segregation would no longer be tolerated in a democratic society. Discrimination was being challenged and defeated by courageous people who were willing to take a stand. For example, the Montgomery Bus Boycott of 1955–56, led by the Reverend Dr. Martin Luther King, Jr., the youthful, new pastor of Dexter Avenue Baptist Church, had helped spark the nonviolent revolution for social change.

A Jim Crow sign on a segregated bus

The boycott had begun when Rosa Parks, an African-American seamstress, boarded a bus after work, paid her fare, and took a seat as she had many times before. But this time, as the bus filled up, she refused to relinquish her seat to a white passenger and stand the rest of the way home. When the bus driver reminded Mrs. Parks that she was breaking the law, she still refused to give up her seat. The bus driver stopped the bus and called the police, and Mrs. Parks was arrested. The rest is history. In protest, blacks, under the leadership of Dr. King, boycotted city buses for over a year, refusing to give in until their demands for justice were met.

In 1960 the civil rights movement was launched from the headquarters of the Southern Christian Leadership Conference (SCLC) in Atlanta. Dr. King had moved there to organize a concentrated effort against segregation in the South.

Dr. King provided the moral and strategic leadership that gave the movement its power and rallied the energy of blacks and whites in the struggle for human dignity, freedom, and justice.

The student protests began in February 1960, when four black students from North Carolina A. & T. College staged a sit-in at a

Greensboro Woolworth's lunch counter. A few days later white students from a neighboring college joined them in their protest, and within a month there were similar demonstrations in Atlanta and Nashville. To coordinate the marches and sit-ins, the Student Nonviolent Coordinating Committee (SNCC) was organized by young activists meeting on the campus of Shaw University in Raleigh, North Carolina.

While all of this was going on, Lorraine was in the process of converting her play into a movie. She was pleased that the story would reach a much wider audience, but she was concerned that Hollywood might distort her work in a movie version and misrepresent her intent. Her script could bring a different image of black people to the silver screen, just as it had to the stage. And at that particular moment in history the accuracy of black images was an important matter of concern to her.

Before the 1960s and except for a few rare exceptions, movies about African Americans had been sparse in number and derogatory in content and portrayal. In most movies they had minor roles — maids, servants, or entertainers playing themselves. Rarely were black characters developed to reflect the full range of human experiences. Hansberry wanted to make sure the quality and integrity of her story was not sacrificed on the big screen. For this reason, she maintained the rights to write the script herself.

In the first draft of the screenplay, Hansberry tried to pull the audience into the Youngers' environment by adding scenes showing Walter Lee on a street corner listening to a radical speech, Lena on the job as a domestic, Travis in school learning about some of the misconceptions about Africa, and Ruth paying double the price for inferior products in a ghetto grocery store.

Columbia Pictures rejected the additions and sent Hansberry back to the drawing board twice with instructions to keep the script close to the Broadway production, but to tone down Beneatha's attack on God, and to delete all the swear words. (Some of the additions were used in the later productions of the play for television.)

Actually, Hansberry was relieved when the screenplay was finally accepted, because she had expected the studio to demand more substantive changes, which she was not willing to make. She was particularly concerned that the studio might ask her to shift the focus of the story or to change her characters' language patterns.

Over the years white writers wrote dialogue for black actors that didn't resemble any known language pattern used among black people. Trying to explain why these false dialects were offensive frustrated Hansberry, as they do most black people, because more often than not, her position was misunderstood, misrepresented, or ignored.

Hansberry never objected to the use of dialect, but she was vehemently opposed to inauthentic representations of it. She knew that African-American dialect was not a flow of ignorant utterances. Black dialect has its own special patterns that originated in slavery and can be traced to West African languages.

Hansberry pointed to producer/director Otto Preminger's version of *Porgy and Bess* as a prime example of Hollywood's exploitation and distortion of black language. She cleverly addressed the issue in the last scene of *Raisin*. When Walter learns that the insurance money has been stolen, he is devastated. He feels his only recourse is to accept Lindner's offer, which he really doesn't want to do. When Mama asks Walter if he's really going to do it, he answers, yes. "Maybe — maybe I'll just get down on my black knees." He does so, much to his family's horror. He continues: "Captain, Mistah, Bossman — (*Groveling and grinning and wringing his hands in profoundly anguished imitation of the slow-witted movie stereotype*). "A-hee-hee-hee! Oh, yassah boss! Yasssssuh! Great White Father, just gi' ussen de money fo' God's sake, and we'd ain't gwine come out deh and dirty up yo' white folks neighborhood . . ."

Walter Lee wouldn't use language in this way; in fact no black person would speak that way except in the movies. Later, when Walter turns Lindner's offer down, he uses African-American idiom that is neither pretentious nor demeaning. It is not standard English, but his

Lorraine Hansberry adapted her play for the film.

words are expressed in the beautiful way Lorraine had heard migrants from the South express themselves.

WALTER

(*A beat; staring at [Lindner]*) And — my father (*With sudden intensity*) My father almost *beat a man to death* once because this man called him a bad name or something, you know what I mean?

LINDNER

(*Looking up, frozen*) No, no I'm afraid I don't —

WALTER

(*A beat. The tension hangs; then Walter steps back from it.*) Yeah. Well — what I mean is that we come from people who had a lot of *pride.* I mean — we are very proud people. And that's my sister over there and she'd going to be a doctor — and we are very proud —

LINDNER

Well — I am sure that is very nice, but —

WALTER

What I am telling you is that we called you over here to tell you that we are very proud and that this — (*Signaling to* TRAVIS) Travis come here. (TRAVIS *crosses and* WALTER *draws him before him facing the man*) This is my son, and he makes the sixth generation our family in this country. And we have all thought about your offer —

LINDNER

Well, good . . . good —

WALTER

And we have decided to move into our house because my father — my father — he earned it for us brick by brick. (MAMA *has her eyes closed and is rocking back and forth as though she were in church, with her head nodding the Amen yes*) We don't want to make no trouble for nobody or fight no causes, and we will try to be good neighbors. And that's *all* we got to say about that. (*He looks the man absolutely in the eyes*) We don't want your money. (*He turns and walks away.*)

The entire cast of the Broadway production was signed to make the movie, which was directed by Daniel Petrie. The film was shot in Chicago and premiered there in 1961. The reviews were mixed. Some critics called it a "masterpiece," while others claimed the movie lost the intimacy of the play. Others claimed the set seemed claustrophobic. One interesting comment came from John Cutts who wrote in *Films and Filming* in 1961:

> *On film, [the movie's] effect is at once less urgent and personal, and one seriously feels the lack of breathing space needed between us, the spectator of the action, and the action itself . . .*

Shot on the small set of an apartment with too many occupants, there *is* a closed-in — claustrophobic — quality to the film, and the tight camera work does destroy the sense of distance between the audience and the actors. What Cutts failed to realize was the tremendous achievement in the set design. The movie succeeds very well in making the viewer feel the lack of space that the family has to endure. The cramped space also magnifies the conflict which is necessary to keep a one-set movie from being boring.

Reviews of this kind didn't dampen black people's enthusiasm for the movie. They went to see it in record numbers. White support for the film was strong, too. *A Raisin in the Sun* was nominated for best screenplay of the year by the Screen Writers Guild.

Hansberry's words and characters provided black actors with material that helped them soar. "It was easy to understand the people we were playing," said Ruby Dee. "They were familiar."

Several of the stars received rave reviews for their work. Sidney Poitier brought an electrifying combination of anger and despair to the role of Walter Lee Younger. (Ossie Davis who followed Poitier on Broadway and Danny Glover who starred in the American Playhouse remake in 1989 also gave sterling performances of Walter Lee Younger.) Poitier's powerful gestures and facial expressions captured the essence of a desperate man — a son, brother, husband, and father — who, at any moment, might explode. "He's just two steps away from that morning when he'll get up and say, 'What the hell. I'll live with it,'" Poitier said, interpreting his character in an interview. "Oh, he'll come close, but he won't give up."

Poitier makes the audience feel Walter Lee's sense of failure as a husband and provider in the scene where he confesses: "I want to hang some real pearls 'round my wife's neck. Ain't she supposed to wear no pearls? Somebody tell me — tell me, who decides which woman is supposed to wear pearls in this world. I tell you I am a *man* — I think my wife should wear some pearls in this world!"

The reviewers also singled out Ruby Dee for her performance as Ruth Younger. Her work on stage and in the movie earned her high praise for being consistent and moving, "a tiny tower of strength and conviction." Reviewers also mentioned how Dee's low-key presence gave the play balance. "Some people mistakenly think Ruth is a weak character," said Dee. "Far from it. She is just as angry as Walter Lee and just as determined as Mama Younger."

"If you've got good dialogue you can act," said Poitier, who also felt that Hansberry's opening dialogue between Walter and Ruth set the standard of excellence for the rest of the script.

WALTER

You look young this morning baby.

RUTH
(*Indifferently*)

Yeah?

WALTER

Just for a second — stirring them eggs. It's done now — just for a second it was — you looked real young again.
(*Then, drily*)
It's gone now. You look like yourself again.

RUTH

(*Setting his eggs before him.*)

Man, if you don't shut up and leave me alone.

WALTER

First thing a man ought to learn in life is not to make love to no colored woman first thing in morning. You all come evil people at eight o'clock in the morning.

The critics felt that Diana Sands was well-cast as Beneatha. "Beneatha was me at age twenty," said Hansberry. The actress had just the perfect blend of youthful vitality and naiveté to make her character believable. Unfortunately Sands died at a very young age, so moviegoers never got to experience the full potential of her talent. Her role as Beneatha is probably the most memorable one of her career.

African-American critics mentioned the timeliness of the movie and praised its themes of perseverance and pride at a time when young blacks were risking their lives in sit-ins all over the country. They also pointed out that millions of blacks were seeing a positive representation of an African on the silver screen. Joseph Asagai, as portrayed by Ivan Dixon, wasn't the typical "Ungawaeh" Hollywood African. (*Ungawaeh* is a made-up word often used in *Tarzan* movies.)

Dixon as Asagai presented the image of a sophisticated man with charm and conviction, a lot like the students Hansberry had met while in college and in New York. She admitted that Asagai, which means "sawed off spear" was her favorite character and that perhaps she had romanticized him a bit for that reason. However, she sincerely believed that he represented "a true intellectual," a nationalist and revolutionary, "realistic enough to know that African leaders may turn out to be as corrupt as their white predecessors, but wise enough to know that before African nations could correct what was wrong with themselves they had to be free first."

The other actors were as commendable in their roles as they had been on stage, making the film worthy of the 1961 Gary Cooper Award for "Outstanding Human Values," at the Cannes Film Festival.

19

While the film was in production, Hansberry worked on *Follow the Drinking Gourd,* a script the National Broadcasting Company (NBC) commissioned her to write as the first in a series of teledramas commemorating the Civil War.

Once again pulling from her own interests and childhood memories, Hansberry chose slavery as her topic. In 1960 most people's image of slavery came from movies like *Gone With the Wind.* Slaves were viewed in one of three, one-dimensional stereotypes: the self-sacrificing servants who put the needs of the master before their own; the silly and childish souls who needed protection; or lazy and shiftless brutes who only answered to the whip.

Hansberry felt slavery was a subject in need of an honest presentation of facts. She chose her title from the spiritual she learned in childhood, "Follow the Drinking Gourd," which was associated with the Underground Railroad, a slave escape system. Hansberry also wanted to correct the misconception about the size of most southern plantations. Most were farms worked by no more than five to ten slaves. The huge estates with hundreds of singing, happy slaves were another Hollywood myth. While there were a few hundred plantations of that size, most of them were broken up into smaller, more manageable farms.

Hansberry's three-act drama is set on the Sweet plantation, a typical cotton farm. The drama opens with a prologue spoken by a black Union soldier who summarizes American slavery from 1619 to the eve of the Civil War.

The main character is Rissa, a slave woman who is owned by Hiram and Maria Sweet. Hansberry introduces Rissa to the audience as a faithful, obedient servant in the *Gone With the Wind* tradition. "Master Sweet" is a rugged individualist who'd started the plantation thirty-five years before with fifty dollars, Rissa, and three other slaves.

Rissa is the Sweets' cook. She wants her son Hannibal to work in the big house with her. In the conversation, Hannibal refuses to accept his bondage. Rissa scolds him and reminds him that things could be worse. She points out that for the most part, Hiram is a decent man who is not unkind to his slaves. She assures him he'll feel better when he's out of the fields and working in the big house. Hannibal can't understand his mother's loyalty to a man who "owns" her, but he doesn't argue with her.

Meanwhile Zeb, a poor white man, had convinced Hiram's son Everett that he can get more work out of the slaves. Hiram doesn't like Zeb, but he lets Everett hire him as the overseer. Zeb beats the slaves to get them to work harder and faster.

Young Tommy Sweet, Hiram's youngest son, teaches Hannibal to read and write, although it is forbidden by law. Hannibal shares his secret with Sarah, the girl he loves and plans to marry.

HANNIBAL
(*smiling*)
What you think I would do with a Bible, Sarah?

> (*She clearly indicates she hasn't the vaguest notion. He waits — then*)

Sarah, I kin read it.

> (SARAH *lifts her head slowly and just looks at him*)

I kin. I kin read, Sarah.

> (SARAH *is speechless as he opens the Bible*)

Listen —

> (*Placing one finger on the page and reading painfully because of the light and the newness of the ability*)

"The — Book — of Jeremiah."

> (*He halts and looks in her face for the wonder which is waiting there*)

> SARAH
> (*Softly, with incredulity*)

Hannibal —

> (*Then, suspiciously*)

You can't make them marks out for real. You done memorized from prayer meetin'.

> HANNIBAL
> (*Laughing gently*)

No, Sarah — "And I said, O, that I had wings like a dove, then would I fly away and be at rest . . ."

> (*He closes the book and looks at her. She stares at him in joy and wonder*)

> SARAH

That's where you go all the time — Somebody been learning you —

> (*With sudden fear*)

Don't you know what they do to you if they finds out?"

[NOTE: The material Hannibal reads is from Psalms and not Jeremiah.]

Sarah's concerns are brought to bear when a slave who is seeking favor with Zeb betrays Hannibal and his secret is discovered. As punishment Everett blinds Hannibal.

Hiram is shocked by his son's cruelty, but blames Zeb whom he orders to leave the plantation immediately. The old master goes to the quarters to find Rissa and beg for her forgiveness, but Rissa turns away from him. When Hiram leaves the cabin he is stricken with a heart attack. He calls out for help. Although she hears him, Rissa vengefully stays inside the cabin, refusing to come to his aid. Hiram dies alone and unattended.

Some weeks later the Civil War begins. Maria Sweet is a widow and her son Everett has joined the Confederate Army. Zeb, who has also joined the Confederates, rides by and mocks them. In the background slaves are singing "Steal Away to Jesus," a spiritual used to communicate that an escape has been planned by the Underground Railroad. In slave songs "heaven" and "Jesus" were sometimes interchangeable with "freedom."

> *"When I get to heaven, (freedom)*
> *gon' put on my shoes and gon'*
> *walk all over God's heaven (freedom).*

Rissa takes her dead master's gun to where Hannibal and Sarah are waiting. Sarah is going to lead blind Hannibal to freedom by following the "Drinking Gourd."

In a 1972 essay, "Lorraine Hansberry's Last Dramas," W. Edward Farrison said that *Follow the Drinking Gourd* was "imaginative, unified, easily documentable," besides being "an intensely interesting story." But unfortunately, the teleplay was rejected in 1961 because the network thought it was too controversial. Producer-director Dore Schary called it "a powerful marvelous script that might have been — with the cast we had in mind and a little luck — one of the great things we've seen on television." Television audiences would have to wait until Alex Haley's *Roots* was produced in 1977 to see the topic of slavery dealt with from a black writer's point of view.

Hollywood had approached Hansberry about writing another script, but she wasn't interested. Hansberry's interest in and desire to write about people of color all over the world led her to accept a project with an independent production company that wanted to make a film based on the Haitian novelist Jacques Roumain's *The Masters of the Dew*.

She was drawn to the project, because she was aware of the parallels between the Africans who were brought to the Caribbean Islands and the United States, but also mindful that while the two groups shared a common history in Africa, they developed different cultures in the Western Hemisphere.

Hansberry produced three drafts of the screenplay, the third of which was polished enough for production. But her clients didn't think so. They sued her for breach of contract and refused to pay for the work she'd done. Hansberry counter-sued, and her lawyers lined up an impressive number of professionals who were willing to testify as to the quality of the screenplay, including Langston Hughes, and the co-translator of the English version of the novel. However, their testimony wasn't necessary, because the case was settled in the judges' chamber in 1963. The movie was never made, and the script is still waiting to be produced.

20

In 1960 Hansberry was considered for a Spingarn Medal, given by the NAACP for an outstanding achievement by an African American, but instead it went to Langston Hughes. Actually, Hansberry didn't mind losing the award to Hughes, but her friend James Baldwin disagreed.

With so much going on in her professional life, it is hard to imagine having enough time to have fun. And one of her favorite things to do was "rap," or converse, with her buddy, James Baldwin.

The debates between Baldwin and Hansberry sometimes continued until three o'clock in the morning, long after other guests had left a gathering at the new brownstone Lorraine had bought on Waverly Place in the Village. Hansberry and Baldwin had things in common: their fear of heights, elevators, bridges, and hospitals, but they disagreed about a number of things, especially the greatness of Hughes.

Baldwin felt he was outdated and overrated, and Hansberry felt Hughes had not been honored enough for his literary contributions. The irony, of course, is that Hughes's work was strong enough — then and now — to endure in spite of Baldwin's criticisms and without Hansberry's defense.

Lorraine Hansberry accepts an honor from Roosevelt University, with her mother and sister Mamie.

But the two young writers had a running dialogue about Hughes that dated back to 1953. Baldwin had written a scathing review in *The New York Times Book Review* on one of Hughes's poetry books. "Every time I read Langston Hughes," Baldwin wrote, "I am amazed all over again by his genuine gifts — and depressed that he has done so little with them." He didn't stop there. Baldwin continued, saying that a more "disciplined poet," would have "thrown many of the poems in the volume in the waste basket."

Hughes, who had been a mentor to so many young writers, was

reportedly crushed by the tone of the review. But more than a few Hughes fans leaped to his defense, including Lorraine, who told a reporter: "Jimmy shows Langston no respect . . . He refers to Langston in public the way we niggers usually talk in private to each other." Perhaps Hansberry had forgotten her own review of Richard Wright's work (he had just died in 1960) while she was at *Freedom,* but Baldwin hadn't forgotten, and he was quick to remind her of it.

By 1961, when both Hansberry and Baldwin were well-known and respected writers facing criticisms of their own, they were finally able to agree that Wright was a genius and Hughes's Spingarn honor was long overdue.

21

In May 1961, a few months after President John F. Kennedy took the oath of office and named his brother Robert F. Kennedy Attorney General, thirteen young blacks and whites began a bus trip through the South to protest the segregation of interstate transportation. To the horror of the world, the bus was stopped and burned in Anniston, Alabama. A mob attacked the Freedom Riders in Birmingham. Robert Kennedy sent four hundred U.S. marshals to Montgomery to restore order. As a result of the freedom rides, however, the Interstate Commerce Commission issued a regulation forbidding segregation on all interstate transportation vehicles and terminals.

All over the country people watched the nightly news in shock and horror. Images of young civil rights demonstrators being brutalized by dogs, slammed into walls by the force of fire hoses, beaten while arrested, and humiliated in jails touched the hearts and minds of Americans everywhere. People who normally wouldn't have become involved in a protest of any kind found themselves bound for the South to join forces with the beleaguered workers. The spiritual

During the Montgomery Bus Boycott, protesters took refuge in their church.

"We Shall Overcome" was the battle cry of the movement and it was sung with a determination that could not be beaten down.

For several years Hansberry had been refining and defining her ideological stance toward the civil rights movement as it was taking shape in the South under the leadership of the Reverend Dr. Martin Luther King, Jr. She had a great deal of respect for Dr. King and what he had been able to accomplish in the South. She knew that ending segregation wouldn't automatically mean equal opportunity. It hadn't worked that way in the North. Northern blacks didn't have Jim Crow laws to protest against, but there were invisible racial barriers that were embedded in the structure of northern housing patterns, educational institutions, and businesses.

In 1962 Hansberry wrote a letter in which she contrasted the nonviolent approach to social change with the more militant methods advocated by some black activists. She believed that nonviolence, while morally inspiring, was not the only option blacks had to fight discrimination. She said black people "must concern themselves with every single means of struggle: legal, illegal, passive, active, violent, and nonviolent . . . I think," Hansberry continued, "Dr. King increasingly will have to face a forthcoming generation of Negroes who question even the restraints of his militant and, currently progressive, ideas and concepts." She also accused the press of lulling "the white community falsely in dismissing the rising temper of the ghetto and what will come of it."

W.E.B. DuBois and Paul Robeson had passed off the scene as leaders of national influence. In 1958, after their passports had been reissued, both Robeson and DuBois had left the country. Robeson toured Europe, the Soviet Union, and China, and DuBois attended an all-African conference in Ghana, where he'd urged African nations to consider socialism over capitalism. Three years later, at the age of 93, DuBois had moved to Ghana where he worked on an encyclopedia of Africa. With these two leaders out of the country and other blacks involved in the Southern movement, there was a void in urban black leadership.

A man who understood the problems of the Northern ghetto and spoke about them eloquently was Malcolm X, a minister in the Nation of Islam, also known as the Black Muslims. He was born Malcolm Little in 1925, but he changed his name to Malcolm X after converting to the Nation of Islam while serving a prison term between 1946 and 1952. During and after slavery, blacks had used their master's last

Malcolm X

name. As an act of establishing their own identity, newly converted Muslims rejected their former names and chose new ones.

Lorraine's first contact with Malcolm X was through *Muhammed Speaks,* a Muslim newspaper he had founded. In 1954 Malcolm X was sent to New York by Elijah Muhammed, leader of the Muslims, to organize a mosque in Harlem. While Martin Luther King, Jr., was chipping away at the stranglehold segregation had on the advancement of Southern blacks, Malcolm was advocating separatism in the North, preaching that whites were inherently evil and America's system of justice was so corrupt that black people needed to live, work, worship, and play separately.

Malcolm's message to black people was about taking control of their own lives. His words empowered them to do something rather than stand by helplessly and allow others to do for them. Harlem youth were impressed with his leadership, because he articulated all their frustrations and offered them solutions that seemed to work. Malcolm's popularity grew partly because of the anger that was sweeping the black urban community. And when he spoke about "uniting to fight a common enemy," he won even more support outside the Muslim religion.

Lorraine and Malcolm had known about each other's work since the years she was at *Freedom* and he was editing *Muhammed Speaks,* but they had never actually met. She wasn't sure she wanted to at first, because she disagreed with him on a number of issues, especially interracial marriages. He stated it was a serious problem among blacks because it split their loyalties. He cited Harry Belafonte, Sammy Davis, Jr., and Lorraine Hansberry in his article.

Lorraine met Malcolm X in 1963, when they happened to attend the same social gathering. A mutual friend, Ossie Davis, introduced them. With eyes flashing, Lorraine cornered Malcolm and told him she resented his harping on her mixed marriage. Malcolm, whose views on that issue had changed by then, was "possibly for the only time in his public career — speechless." Davis remembered him laughing and stammering. Afterwards, he and Hansberry became "friends in the cause."

Hansberry remained keenly aware of and interested in Africa all of her life. She was a Pan-Africanist and intensely concerned about the problems emerging black countries were experiencing, especially when it was suggested that there was American interference in the development of these new nations. Patrice Lumumba, a leader in the newly formed country of the Congo, was murdered in 1961 and there were strong implications that the United States Central Intelligence Agency (CIA) might have been involved. A group of African Americans, enraged by the murder of an African leader, staged a protest at the United Nations Security Council.

Nobel Peace Prize winner Dr. Ralph Bunche, who was at that time Under-Secretary to the United Nations, apologized for the behavior of his fellow blacks. When Hansberry heard about Bunche's apology, she responded in an open letter, published by *The New York Times*. She wrote in part:

> *As so many of us were shocked and outraged as reports of Dr. Ralph Bunche's "apologies" for the demonstrators, we were also curious as to his mandate from our people to do so. In the face of it and, on apparently as much authority, I hasten to apologize to Mme. Pauline Lumumba and the Congolese people for our Dr. Bunche.*

Suddenly, and without seeking it, Hansberry had become a leading voice in the civil rights movement.

22

In 1962 Lorraine and Robert bought a house in Croton-on-Hudson, which Lorraine jokingly called "Chitlin' Heights." The full glass walls opened on to a deep wooded area. The house reminded Lorraine of the lecture she'd attended by Frank Lloyd Wright, the famous architect who insisted that good design should make artificial spaces work harmoniously with nature.

Hansberry's journal entry for October 1, 1962 said:

> *I have arranged the work space after the advice of Leonardo; large airy house (Not too large) with small, compact, rather crowded even, work area: desk, machine, drawing board hem me in. I love it. It is as I wish it.*

Her writing space was a bright, sunny place, cheerfully decorated with randomly placed art, personal notes, and photographs of Paul Robeson and Michelangelo's David. At her shoulder was the bust of

Lorraine Hansberry's office
in her new home

Einstein, and at the top of her stairs was one of her favorite playwright, O'Casey. Looking around at the things in her office, she wrote
in her journal:

*The company I keep! But — just to keep things in perspective — I have
made me a rather large reminder which is now tacked in the most prominent place of all. It reads: "BUT — " SAID THE CHILD — "THE EM-
PEROR ISN'T WEARING ANY CLOTHES" . . .*

While sipping coffee and chain-smoking, she sat at her typewriter
for long stretches, writing with a consuming sense of urgency.

The play she'd been working on was *The Sign in Jenny Reed's Window* which she later retitled, *The Sign in Sidney Brustein's Window*. While working on it steadily, she still found time to draw up plans for a community theater project in Harlem, to be called the John Brown Memorial Theater, named in honor of the abolitionist who tried to lead a slave revolt at Harper's Ferry, Virginia (now West Virginia). Brown was hanged in 1859. Hansberry's choice of name and the goals she listed for the theater clearly reflect her world view of art.

One of her goals for the theater was that it would

> *draw its main source from the life of the Negro people and their allies . . . Toward these ends, then, let all artists of grand imagination and skills be welcomed here! Let the myriad artists of all peoples be represented here: let all who find a poetic word in behalf of the human race and that of its portion which is, in particular — black, be welcome here . . . Let the arts renounce all tyranny in this place . . .*

Unfortunately, the theater project never materialized, but performing groups across the country have incorporated many of the concepts she set forth as a dramatist who believed in "the oneness of the cause of humanity."

23

The 1963 publication of Betty Friedan's book *The Feminine Mystique* has been credited by many as the beginning of the modern women's movement, but Lorraine Hansberry had been a feminist long before it became a movement.

Hansberry had never accepted the narrowly defined role of women as homemakers, mothers, and sex objects. During the Studs Terkel interview, Hansberry said she had been influenced by African-American women activists such as Harriet Tubman, Sojourner Truth,

Mary Church Terrell, Ida B. Wells-Barnett, and Mary McLeod Bethune. "Obviously," Hansberry said, "the most oppressed group of any oppressed people will be its women who are twice oppressed . . . So, as oppression makes people more militant, women become twice militant, because they are twice oppressed."

Although Hansberry fought all her life against the traditional roles set for women, she was not anti-male. She even acknowledged that there were some men, like Frederick Douglass, for example, who were capable of defending women's rights. In an unpublished essay dated 1957, Hansberry stated that "if by some miracle women should not ever utter a single protest against their condition there would still exist among men those who could not endure in peace until their liberation be achieved."

Hansberry talking to youth in a summer camp in New York State

Through her own analysis of sexism as it existed in the 1950s and early 1960s, Hansberry came to believe mothers perpetuated sexism by teaching their daughters that they should be wives instead of career women. "And if they had to work by necessity then they should be teachers and not principals, nurses and not doctors, and secretaries and not managers."

Had she lived, she would have no doubt been a spokesperson for the new generation of women who would not accept second-class citizenship willingly, and who, in her own words

would be forever in ferment and agitation against their condition and what they understand to be their oppressors. If not by overt rebellion or revolution, then in the thousand and one ways they will devise with and without consciousness to alter their condition.

Although Hansberry's views about homosexuality were not a primary part of her activism, she stated in an unsigned article in *The Ladder,* a lesbian publication, that "homosexual persecution" had at its roots not only social ignorance, but sexism as well.

Lorraine Hansberry's sexuality has been the topic of much debate. Was she a lesbian? During her lifetime, she chose not to discuss her sexuality publicly, and until more of Hansberry's writings are made public and the research about her life more carefully and thoughtfully conducted, it is impossible to say much more about that subject.

24

1963.

Lorraine began the year hopeful. She wrote:

For the New Year I have only two resolutions and I know that they are ones I will keep — because I have to: I shall write and I shall train Chaka, my German Shepherd puppy. Beyond these things let life bring what it will —

25

1963 was a pivotal year in the civil rights movement. Eugene "Bull" Connor, the Police Commissioner of Birmingham, Alabama, used fire hoses and dogs against demonstrators, many of them children. Thousands of protesters were arrested and beaten. Thousands more joined the movement to support SCLC and SNCC marches and voter registration drives. Others who couldn't come sent money, held fundraisers, or wrote letters to their congressmen.

Hansberry watched the events unfold as she continued to work on several major projects including a play about her childhood hero, the liberator of Haiti, Toussaint L'Ouverture, and two other plays. But after several dizzy spells she went to see a doctor in April. "Results:" she wrote, "Sick girl. Hospital on the 20th. Enjoying the attention mightily."

On May 1, 1963, she wrote to a young playwright she had been mentoring, "they have discovered that I have ulcers and anemia and here I am. Nothing serious, but enough to keep me out of action for a bit."

Actually, Lorraine was much sicker that anybody knew at that point. Further tests revealed that she *probably* had cancer of the duodenum, which is part of the intestinal tract. To know more conclusively, a panel of physicians suggested surgery, which a second opinion confirmed.

"When I heard her small voice on the telephone," said Mamie, "I knew something terrible was wrong. Of course, Mother and I went to New York immediately. The first operation verified what the doctors had suspected. Lorraine had cancer, but they were hopeful that during the operation most of the cancerous tissue had been removed."

For a while Lorraine regained her strength and continued her writing. At the same time she was struggling for her life, African Americans were battling for the life of the civil rights movement. Instead of allowing her illness to impede her action, Hansberry drew strength from her commitment.

On May 24 — just weeks after being diagnosed with cancer — Lorraine Hansberry, along with James Baldwin, performers Harry Belafonte and Lena Horne, the actor Rip Torn, Ed Berry of the Chicago Urban League, sociologist Dr. Kenneth Clark, and Jerome Smith, a member of SNCC, met Robert Kennedy and his aide, Burke Marshall, to discuss their views on civil rights issues.

James Baldwin, who had pushed for the meeting, was asked to select those who would attend the "informal gathering at a New York hotel." All the attendees there had their own version of what happened, but most agreed that the meeting began with the usual exchange of platitudes. The group petitioned Kennedy to encourage the President to strengthen his program regarding civil rights and to provide help for the civil rights activists who were putting their lives on the line to help people register to vote.

A few statistics were batted around, then to everyone's surprise, Jerome Smith, the young SNCC worker, exclaimed, "Okay, let's cut through the bull." Smith spoke passionately about the brutal beatings that were taking place in Birmingham where he was stationed and throughout the South. Justice, he said, was a joke in rural Mississippi where the Klan ruled by fear and brutality. He spoke about the rights of blacks whose homes, churches, and businesses were systematically torched if they dared try to register to vote, attend a SNCC meeting, or even give shelter to a SNCC worker. Smith demanded to know what the Attorney General of the United States planned to do about these kinds of injustices?

Smith wasn't a polished or tactful speaker, but his words were powerful and emboldened the others who began speaking their minds. The tone of the talks shifted. Baldwin accused the Kennedy Administration of dragging its feet with regard to civil rights legislation. The Attorney General argued that the administration had a strong record on civil rights, which was true, but judged by the immediacy of the need, its actions did seem timid.

Someone suggested the Kennedys didn't want to move too fast with regard to civil rights because they feared losing Southern voters.

Baldwin said, "We wanted him to tell his brother, the President, to personally escort to school, on the following day . . . a small black girl already scheduled to enter a Deep South school. That way, it will be clear that whoever spits on that child will be spitting on the nation." Kennedy seemed confounded by the request and responded: "The President can't be responsible for walking a child to school." He missed the point.

According to several Kennedy documents, Kennedy's aide, Burke Marshall, is reported to have said during an interview in 1965 that the group "thought the President should have sent the Army to Birmingham. They wouldn't listen to any rational discussion of what it would do there or what the problem was in Birmingham."

For most of the meeting, Hansberry had been an observer, taking in all the words and emotions that had been vented around her. Baldwin said Lorraine's face, "changed and changed, the way Sojourner Truth's face must have changed and changed . . . [Lorraine] wanted him to hear her." When Kennedy missed the point that Baldwin was trying to make, she leaned forward, looked at the Attorney General directly in his eyes and said, "We would like from you a moral commitment."

Kennedy remembered it differently. "Lorraine Hansberry said that they were going to go down and get guns, and they were going to give the guns to people on the street, and they were going to start to kill white people. They kept talking about — let's see — the white people were castrating the Negroes. You know, it was all that kind of conversation — in poetical terms — about the position of the Negro . . ."

Kennedy felt he had lost control of the meeting and he seemed to take everything that was said personally. Tempers flared. Loyalty to the country was questioned. Then suddenly, Lorraine stood, silently put on her coat, and walked out. "Her face was a strange mixture of anger and hurt," said Baldwin. "We were getting nowhere, so what was the point of staying?" she told Baldwin later.

The press made much more out of the meeting than there was to make. Headlines claimed that the meeting turned into a shouting match. Kennedy commented that the people at the meeting had "complexes about the fact that they've been successful. I mean, that they'd done so well and this poor boy had been beaten by the police. Others had been beaten and they hadn't been beaten . . . So the way to show that they hadn't forgotten where they came from was to berate me and berate the United States government . . ."

The Kennedy administration was extremely popular among black Southerners, so when the news of the meeting reached the public, Baldwin, Hansberry, and the others were sharply criticized for possibly alienating the President and the Attorney General by their "militancy." Some people even began distancing themselves from the more militant faction of SNCC. There were others, however, who pointed out that nothing so out of the ordinary had been said at the meeting. Civil rights leaders and organizations had been asking for justice and equality for centuries. James Baldwin said the problem was, the people in the meeting weren't "begging" for their rights. They made "demands," and "white people don't like it when black people stand up for themselves and make demands," Baldwin said.

Hansberry avoided making comments about the meeting to the press because she didn't want the media hype to divert attention from the real problems the civil rights volunteers were having with the SNCC voter registration drive.

Several months after the Kennedy meeting, Hansberry did speak about the event at a fund-raiser at a synagogue in Croton-on-Hudson along with Jerome Smith. "I think," she said, "we have all, perhaps to the point of exhaustion, heard of the recent meeting that some people, myself and Mr. Smith among them, had with the Attorney General of the United States." Although many of their comments had been quoted, Hansberry said she wanted to quote one of her own. "After the Attorney General had shown impatience, I suggested," Hansberry said, "that Mr. Kennedy re-examine his impatience," because in the struggle for freedom, black people were united. "What we are interested in is in making perfectly clear that between Negro intelligentsia, the Negro middle class, and the Negro this-and-that — we are one people. And that as far as we are concerned, we are represented by the Negroes in the streets of Birmingham!"

Hansberry was prepared to help the volunteers in any way she could and that included sending weapons if they needed them. But for the moment, the movement was only in need of an automobile.

The money they raised that day was used to buy a station wagon for the SNCC offices in Philadelphia, Mississippi. The following year, three civil rights workers, James E. Chaney, Michael Schwerner, and Andrew Goodman, were kidnapped from *that* vehicle. Their bodies were not found until months later, but the brutal murders had a galvanizing effect on the civil rights workers. Northern whites who had been somewhat apathetic to the cause were enraged that America's children were being murdered for apparently no other reason than trying to get people to vote. The press flocked to Mississippi and stories about the three deaths filled the pages of newspapers all over the

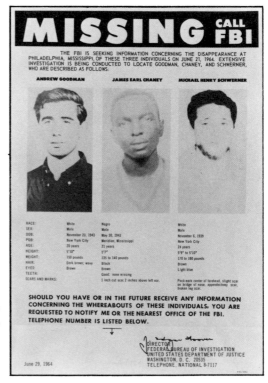

The FBI poster for Andrew Goodman, James Chaney, and Michael Schwerner

country. Lorraine mourned the loss of life — all life. "Schwerner and Goodman are the exception in Mississippi, but Chaney is the rule," she told a friend. What she meant was that Schwerner and Goodman were Northern whites who were murdered by white supremacists, but Chaney, who was black, lived under the threat of being lynched daily.

Lorraine's health deteriorated rapidly and she was in constant pain. While most of her friends were attending the famous March on Washington, August 28, 1963, Lorraine was preparing for another surgery. She sat up to hear Martin Luther King's historic "I Have a Dream" speech from her hospital room in Boston. She predicted that it would be a speech often remembered and quoted.

In Washington, more than 250,000 blacks and whites from every region and from every socio-economic level imaginable came to the nation's capital to show their support for equal rights, more jobs, and the speedy passage of civil rights legislation. It was announced at the March on Washington, that the day before, Hansberry's friend and teacher Dr. W.E.B. DuBois had died in Ghana at the age of 95. The sad irony, of course, was that many of the young civil rights volunteers who were there that day didn't even know who DuBois was or that their work was a fulfillment of his dream.

The March sent a powerful message to Congress and President Kennedy. The President didn't waste any time. He promised to push for passage of a bill that was before the House, and several senators added their support.

In the fall of 1963, when everything was dying, Hansberry was told that she was dying, too. Her prognosis was terminal and the civil rights movement was facing its darkest hour as well. Medgar W. Evers, NAACP field secretary in Mississippi and a World War II hero, had been gunned down in his front yard by a white assassin on June 12, 1963. Four little girls were killed on September 15, 1963, when they arrived early for Sunday School at Birmingham's Sixteenth Street Baptist Church and a bomb exploded. Then on November 22, 1963, John F. Kennedy was assassinated in Dallas, Texas.

Mercifully 1963 ended.

26

January 1964. A new year had begun, but old problems persisted. Lorraine's health continued to fail, but she managed to write regularly in spite of the pain that drained her strength.

Hansberry had been working on *The Sign in Sidney Brustein's Window* off and on since 1961, but she was pleased with its progress. Hansberry returned to it, taxing herself to the limits of her endurance to complete it. "Without her work she would have died sooner," said Mamie. "She seemed to turn a corner with the play." Lorraine thought so, too.

"The work goes superbly!" she wrote. "Yes: Sidney Brustein! His character for the first time — beckons feeling from us! I am pleased. And certain of his speeches now — they transcend themselves and become good language of the theater. I am anxious to get on to *Toussaint* soon — only death or infirmity can stop me now . . ."

The characters in *Sidney Brustein's Window* are very different from those in *Raisin*. They are based on people Hansberry knew from the old neighborhood in the Village. The main character, Sidney Brustein, a Jewish intellectual, is weighed down by the struggle between wanting not to care and caring too much. Hansberry deals with homosexuality, racism, anti-Semitism, politics, prostitution, psychoanalysis, marriage, business, and art, and for that reason, the play has been called "too complicated." Nevertheless she finished it and it was put into production right away.

27

In March 1964 Robert and Lorraine secretly divorced. There has been a great deal of speculation about why the couple separated, but neither of them discussed the reasons publicly. Only their families and very close friends knew, because Robert continued to work with Lorraine every day. She even named Robert her literary executor in her will, a responsibility he fulfilled until his death in 1991.

Lorraine's health continued to fail, but she managed to write regularly in spite of the pain that drained her strength.

Between hospital visits for radiation treatment, Hansberry worked on the text for *The Movement*, a photo documentary of the civil rights struggle, prepared with the help of SNCC.

Hansberry opened the book with a quotation from Baldwin:

It is a terrible and inexorable law that one cannot deny the humanity of another without diminishing one's own.

One of the most stunning pictures in the book is a photograph by Danny Lyons in which three unnamed protesters are kneeling in front of the city hall of Cairo, Illinois. Lyons captured the spirit of determination of those on the front-line of the civil rights movement.

The disease had taken its toll on Lorraine's small frame. She was thin and very weak, yet, on Monday, March 17, she participated in a forum known as "the Town Hall" meeting, along with actors Ossie Davis, Ruby Dee, and writers Paule Marshall, John Killens, and Amiri Baraka.

Although some of the other participants didn't agree with her, Hansberry believed that a dialogue between the races was essential before any concrete societal changes could take place in the American racial impasse. She didn't think it was necessary to eliminate whites from participating in the movement, but she wanted them to be firmly committed.

Some of the other speakers expressed their anger and frustration, and they mistrusted the intent of white liberals who were full of rhetoric but short on action. Remaining true to her own convictions, Hansberry made her position clear when she said:

The problem is we have to find some way, with these dialogues, to encourage the white liberal to stop being liberal — and become an American rad-

ical. Radicalism is not alien to this country, neither black nor white. We have a very great tradition of white radicalism in the United States — and I've never heard Negroes boo the name of John Brown. Some of the first people who have died so far in this struggle have been white men . . . I don't think we can decide ultimately on the basis of color. The passion that we express should be understood, I think, in that context. We want total identification. It's not a question of reading anybody out; it's a merger . . . but it has to be a merger on the basis of true and genuine equality. And if we think that it isn't going to be painful, we're mistaken.

She concluded the evening with her most quoted statement (often by people who don't know the source): "It is no longer acceptable to allow racists to define black manhood — and it will have to come to pass that they can no longer define his weaponry."

In retrospect Hansberry's comments seem so rational, it is difficult to understand why she was considered a radical. Many who labeled her radical or "an extremist" would have been surprised with her very level assessment of the Forum: "turned out to be explosive. Negroes are so angry and white people are so confused and sensitive to criticism — but aren't we all?"

June began the long, violent summer of 1964, when riots erupted in major cities across America. Hansberry's beloved Harlem exploded on July 18, 1964, and for five days black people vented all their pent-up anger and frustration by burning, looting, and shooting. Rioting spread to the Bedford-Stuyvesant section of Brooklyn. And on July 25 riots took place in Rochester, New York. Governor Nelson Rockefeller called out the National Guard, but the long, hot summer did not end until riots ripped through several other major Northern cities.

In response to the nonviolent revolution in the South and the violent eruptions in the North, Lorraine examined her own feelings. "Do I remain a revolutionary?" she wrote introspectively. "Without a doubt . . . *Comfort* has come to be its own corruption. I think of lying without a painkiller in pain. In all the young years no such image ever occurred to me. I rather *looked forward* to going to jail once. Now, I can hardly imagine surviving it at all. Comfort . . . I think when I get my health back I shall go into the South to find out what kind of revolutionary I am . . ."

28

There were so many things Hansberry wanted to do, but time was running out. Production on *The Sign in Sidney Brustein's Window* had begun. In October Lorraine and a private nurse moved into the Hotel Abby Victoria, so she could be near rehearsals.

A scene from *The Sign in Sidney Brustein's Window*

The play opened at the Longacre Theater on October 15, 1964, to mixed reviews. Those who expected a play similar to *A Raisin in the Sun* were either pleasantly surprised or terribly confused. One critic who obviously connected with Hansberry's ideas wrote, "I shall never, as long as I live, hope to see such perfection in the theater again . . ." but another critic trashed the writing, plotting, and characters, saying "that, for sheer implausibility, [the play] should win some sort of award."

Most of the reviews were not that extreme. Since it was the first time a black playwright had chosen to write using all white characters, many critics didn't know what to say about it. Some felt that by writing about white Villagers, Lorraine had deserted the causes that concerned black people. They missed the point that Hansberry was trying to make: people could only make a difference if they are committed to something, whether it is work, art, a cause, a belief, or even another person. But more specifically, white liberals had to do more than talk about equality, justice, freedom, and an end to discrimination. They had to become involved — totally committed.

29

After opening night in October, Robert knew *Brustein* was in trouble. Normally it would have closed, but for Lorraine's sake, friends rallied to keep the play open. Actresses Shelley Winters and Ruby Dee championed the cause on radio, television, and in public platforms. In the months that followed people gave time and money to help keep the play open, including James Baldwin, Sammy Davis, Jr., Ossie Davis, Alan Alda, Mel Brooks, Anne Bancroft, Claudia McNeil, Diana Sands, and even Robert F. Kennedy.

Lorraine was admitted to University Hospital the day after the play opened. She had lost her sight and had lapsed into a coma.

Mamie came from California in order to be with her sister. The family had relocated there when their real estate business in Chicago had failed. "That was such a terrible time for us," said Mamie. "Mother wasn't well herself. Oh, how we wanted to do something, but nothing could be done — not to save her that is, but we — Robert and I — tried to keep [Lorraine] from being so frightened. She was so scared when she came out of the coma." Either Robert or Mamie sat with Lorraine all the time.

Over the next few weeks Lorraine's condition improved a little and she even regained her sight. A surprise visit from Uncle Leo in November lifted her spirits. He was home from an extended visit to Africa, and she was eager to talk to him about the new independent African countries that had gained their nationhood, such as Malawi and Kenya where Jomo Kenyatta had emerged through the strife to become the first leader. When he left, Lorraine felt much better, knowing that Africa was becoming a free continent again.

The Sign in Sidney Brustein's Window moved to Henry Miller's Theater on December 22. That Christmas, Robert and Mamie celebrated

The Sign in Sidney Brustein's Window
lasted for 101 performances

at the bedside of Lorraine. "The nurses were wonderful to her," said Mamie. "They sang to her, then after that we exchanged gifts." Robert gave Lorraine a gold and amber necklace. She smiled in appreciation.

Even in those final days, in her weakened condition, Lorraine never missed the opportunity to laugh. Living was so hard, but she was afraid of dying. On the morning of January 12, 1965, Lorraine woke up and seemed to be in good spirits. Then she slipped into a coma and at 8:50 A.M., Lorraine Hansberry died at the age of thirty-four. That night, after 101 performances, the curtain fell on *The Sign in Sidney Brustein's Window* for the last time.

Lorraine's funeral services were held at a small church in Harlem, presided over by the Reverend Eugene Callender, on January 15, 1965. The wooden coffin draped in white flowers was in keeping with her wishes for a simple service.

The congregation sang, "Abide With Me," after which the Reverend Callender read messages from James Baldwin, who was in France, and Martin Luther King, Jr., who said, "Her creative ability and her profound grasp of the deep social issues confronting the world today will remain an inspiration to generations yet unborn."

Following the eulogy, Paul Robeson, who had returned to the United States, made a few remarks. In attendance that day were Langston Hughes, Harry Belafonte, and Malcolm X. Malcolm had changed his name to El Hajj Malik el-Shabazz after his pilgrimage to Mecca, followed by visits to several African capitals. He would be assassinated a few weeks later. And within the year both Nannie Hansberry and Leo Hansberry would also die.

In spite of a raging snowstorm, Hansberry's remains were taken to Croton-on-Hudson where she was buried. Her gravestone is shaped in the form of an open book. The inscription on it is the last line from *The Sign in Sidney Brustein's Window.*

TOMORROW, WE SHALL MAKE SOMETHING STRONG OF THIS SORROW.

30

Lorraine Hansberry was an artist and an activist who would probably like to be remembered as an honest writer, one who tried to be truthful to her audience and to her own beliefs. To safeguard the integrity of her work, she named Robert Nemiroff her literary executor. And except for the time he took to write his own play, *Postmark Zero*, Nemiroff devoted his life to that task. He said:

> As her literary executor . . . with sole responsibility for the future of . . . an important and quite possibly major literary and historical resource, I felt it incumbent upon me to do what I could to see that, insofar as possible, those works that merited it were edited and adapted for production in the media for which they were intended, and that the papers were organized, edited, annotated, and published for the use of the current generation as well as future scholars.

Lorraine left behind many unfinished projects in various stages of completion from concept statement to finished manuscripts. Nemiroff, himself a capable writer, completed Hansberry's play, *Les Blancs,* which opened on Broadway, starring James Earl Jones. Later, Nemiroff and others produced *Raisin,* based on *A Raisin in the Sun,* which won a Tony Award in 1973 for best Broadway musical.

Probably the most enduring work of the Hansberry-Nemiroff collaboration is *To Be Young, Gifted and Black.* First produced in 1968–69 as an off-Broadway play, it ran for nineteen months at the Cherry Lane Theater. The book by the same title was published in 1969, and included an introduction by James Baldwin. In the foreword of the first edition, Nemiroff described *To Be Young, Gifted and Black* as a "portrait of an individual, the workbook of an artist, and the chronicle of a rebel who celebrated the human spirit. It is also, I believe, a prophetic chapter in the history of a people and an age."

The phrase, "young, gifted and black" was so popular at the time,

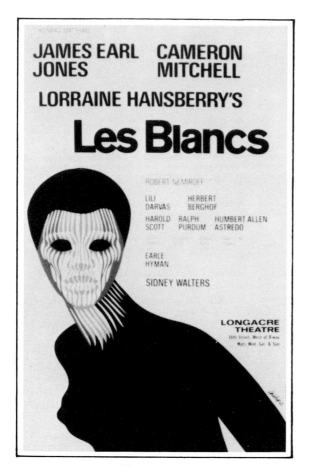

The posters for *Les Blancs* and *To Be Young, Gifted and Black*

it became a song and even entered the language as an affirmation of black pride. Nemiroff chose the title from a speech Lorraine had given to the winners of the United Negro College Fund scholarship contest in May 1964. Though very ill, Lorraine insisted that she give the speech. Her message still has the power to inspire and challenge every new generation that hears her words:

> . . . . *though it be a thrilling and marvelous thing to be merely young and gifted in such times, it is doubly so, doubly dynamic, to be young, gifted* and black!

Lorraine Hansberry

TIMELINE

1930

Lorraine Hansberry is born. *Sinclair Lewis wins the Nobel Prize for Literature.*

1930-1936

Lorraine spends the first years of her life at 5330 Calumet Street on the South Side of Chicago.

1932

Carl and Nannie Hansberry support the Republican ticket, but the Democrat Franklin D. Roosevelt is elected President of the United States. *Bill "Bojangles" Robinson stars in* Harlem Is Heaven, *the first all-black talking movie.*

1934

Carl Hansberry develops a thriving real estate business on Chicago's South Side. *Elijah Muhammad becomes the leader of the Nation of Islam and moves the headquarters to Chicago.*

1935

Lorraine Hansberry begins school at Betsy Ross Elementary. *Zora Neale Hurston publishes* Mules and Men. *George Gershwin's* Porgy and Bess *premieres in New York.*

1936

President Franklin D. Roosevelt establishes the Office of Minority Affairs and appoints Mary McLeod Bethune its administrator. Jesse Owens wins four Olympic gold medals in Germany.

1937

The Hansberry family moves into an all-white neighborhood. An angry mob attacks their home. A state judge rules that the Hansberrys have to move. Hansberry appeals to the Supreme Court. *Zora Neale Hurston publishes* Their Eyes Were Watching God.

1938

The boxer Joe Louis wins the heavyweight championship by defeating Max Schmeling.

1939

Nazi Germany invades Poland.

1940

Supreme Court rules in favor of Hansberry. Carl Hansberry runs for Congress on the Republican ticket and loses by a wide margin. *Richard Wright publishes* Native Son.

1941

In Germany Jews are forced to wear the Star of David. After pressure from black leaders, President Roosevelt issues Executive Order 8802 which forbids racial and religious discrimination in government contracts. Japanese planes attack Pearl Harbor on Sunday, December 7. The United States enters World War II.

1942

Perry and Nannie Hansberry are charter members of the Congress on Racial Equality (CORE).

1943

Perry Hansberry, Jr., is drafted into the military under protest. *Paul Robeson is the first black actor to play* Othello *opposite a white woman. W.E.B. DuBois is the first black scholar admitted to the National Institute of Arts and Letters.*

1944

Lorraine finishes grade school and enters Englewood High School.

1945

Carl Hansberry purchases home in Palanco, Mexico. *President Franklin D. Roosevelt dies. World War II ends. United Nations founded in San Francisco. Three of the founding delegates are African Americans: Walter White of the NAACP, Mary McLeod Bethune, and W.E.B. DuBois.*

1946

Carl Hansberry dies on March 7.

1947

Jackie Robinson joins the Brooklyn Dodgers and becomes first African American to play major league baseball in the 20th century.

1948

Lorraine graduates from Englewood High School and immediately enters the University of Wisconsin. *President Harry S. Truman issues an executive order integrating all branches of the United States military.*

1949

Lorraine studies art in Mexico. *A riot prevents Paul Robeson from performing in Peekskill, New York.*

1950

In February Lorraine leaves the University of Wisconsin and studies at Roosevelt University in Chicago during the summer. In the fall she leaves for New York City. *Gwendolyn Brooks awarded the Pulitzer Prize for* Annie Allen. *Ralph Bunche awarded the Nobel Prize for Peace.*

1951

Lorraine works for *Freedom,* published by Paul Robeson. Meets Robert Nemiroff at demonstration.

1952

Lorraine attends Intercontinental Peace Congress in Montevideo, Uruguay. *Ralph Ellison's novel* Invisible Man *is published.*

1953

Lorraine marries Robert Nemiroff in June. *The Rosenbergs are executed for espionage. James Baldwin publishes his novel* Go Tell It on the Mountain.

1954

Lorraine takes courses from Dr. W.E.B. DuBois at Jefferson School of Social Science. *The U.S. Supreme Court rules that "segregation is inherently unequal and thus unconstitutional" in* Brown vs. Board of Education of Topeka, Kansas.

1955

Lorraine and Robert live in the Village. *Marian Anderson becomes first black to sing at the Metropolitan Opera House in New York. Rosa Parks is arrested for refusing to give up her bus seat to a white passenger.*

1956

Robert Nemiroff sells pop song "Cindy, Oh Cindy." *Rev. Dr. Martin Luther King, Jr., becomes primary leader of the civil rights movement.*

1957

Lorraine finishes play called *The Crystal Stair.* She changes its name to *A Raisin in the Sun. Martin Luther King, Jr., organizes the Southern Christian Leadership Council (SCLC). Ghana becomes first African nation to win its independence from a colonial power.*

1958

A Raisin in the Sun goes into production with Lloyd Richards as director. *Alvin Ailey founds the Alvin Ailey Dance Theater in New York City.*

1959

A Raisin in the Sun opens on Broadway. Lorraine receives the New York Drama Critics Circle Award.

1960

Lorraine writes screenplay for *A Raisin in the Sun. Students hold "sit-ins" in Greensboro, NC. Senator John F. Kennedy elected President of the United States, the first Catholic to hold the office.*

1961

Movie version of *A Raisin in the Sun* premieres in Chicago. *Leroi Jones (Amiri Baraka) publishes first book,* Preface to a Twenty Volume Suicide Note. *The "Freedom Rides" begin. W.E.B. DuBois moves to Ghana.*

1962

Lorraine and Robert buy house in Croton-on-Hudson, New York. *U.S. Supreme Court orders University of Mississippi to admit James H. Meredith. James Baldwin publishes* Another Country. *Jackie Robinson becomes the first black inducted into the Baseball Hall of Fame.*

1963

Lorraine diagnosed with cancer. *Medgar Evers killed in Jackson, Mississippi. More than 200,000 people attend the March on Washington where Dr. Martin Luther King, Jr., gives his "I Have A Dream" speech. Four girls are killed in the bombing of the Sixteenth Street Baptist Church in Birmingham, Alabama. President John F. Kennedy assassinated in Dallas, Texas.*

1964

In March Robert and Lorraine quietly divorce. *The bodies of three civil rights workers found in Philadelphia, Mississippi. Dr. Martin Luther King, Jr., wins the Nobel Peace Prize. Sidney Poitier wins Oscar for* Lilies of the Field.

1965

Lorraine Hansberry dies. *Malcolm X assassinated.*